Nmap® 6 Cookbook
The Fat-free Guide to Network Scanning

NmapCookbook.com

ISBN: 1507781385
EAN-13: 978-1507781388

- BSD® is a registered trademark of the University of California, Berkeley
- CentOS is property of CentOS Ltd.
- Debian® is a registered trademark of Software in the Public Interest, Inc.
- Fedora® is a registered trademark of Red Hat, Inc.
- Linux® is the registered trademark of Linus Torvalds
- Mac OS X® is a registered trademark of Apple, Inc.
- Windows® is a registered trademark of Microsoft Corporation
- Nmap® is a registered trademark of Insecure.Com LLC
- Red Hat® is a registered trademark of Red Hat, Inc.
- Ubuntu® is a registered trademark of Canonical Ltd.
- UNIX® is a registered trademark of The Open Group

All other trademarks used in this book are property of their respective owners. Use of any trademark in this book does not constitute an affiliation with or endorsement from the trademark holder.

All information in this book is presented on an "as-is" basis. No warranty or guarantee is provided and the author and/or publisher shall not be held liable for any loss or damage.

Revision History

Nmap Cookbook, 2010 - Covers Nmap 5

Nmap 6 Cookbook, 2015 - Covers Nmap 6, Nping, Ncat, and other new features plus corrections and expanded content

Copyright © 2015 Nicholas Marsh - All rights reserved.

Dedication

This guide is dedicated to the open source community. Without the tireless efforts of open source developers, programs like Nmap would not exist. Many of these developers devote large amounts of their spare time creating and supporting wonderful open source applications and ask for nothing in return.

The collaborative manner in which open source software is developed shows the true potential of humanity if we all work together towards a common goal.

About Fat Free Publishing

Fat Free Publishing was created with the goal of simplifying highly technical topics into an easily digestible reading format. We don't write overpriced 500-page "bibles" or books for "dummies". We believe that most technology students and professionals' needs fall somewhere in the middle of the spectrum and our titles specifically target that audience.

You will find that our books are simple, yet insightful. We achieve this by writing highly organized guides that avoid "bloat" and "fluff" such as excessive wordiness and obscure use cases. Each Fat Free Guide is designed to get you up to speed quickly, regardless of your knowledge of the topic.

About the Author (Nicholas Marsh)

I have over 15 years of IT experience in a wide array of technologies including Unix/Linux, Windows, networking, and virtualization. I've worked for companies large and small, engineering solutions to meet their ever-changing technology needs.

I write Fat Free Guides for fun. I hope you find my books helpful in expanding your technical knowledge.

Please send questions and comments to nick@fatfreepublishing.com.

Thanks for reading,

Nick Marsh

Contents at a Glance

Introduction 13

Conventions Used In This Book 16

Section 0: Internet Protocol Suite 17

Section 1: Installing Nmap 31

Section 2: Basic Scanning Techniques 45

Section 3: Discovery Options 61

Section 4: Advanced Scanning Options 79

Section 5: Port Scanning Options 89

Section 6: Operating System and Service Detection 99

Section 7: Timing Options 107

Section 8: Evading Firewalls 125

Section 9: Output Options 135

Section 10: Troubleshooting and Debugging 141

Section 11: Zenmap 151

Section 12: Nmap Scripting Engine (NSE) 165

Section 13: Ndiff 175

Section 14: Nping 179

Section 15: Ncat 195

Section 16: Tips and Tricks 203

Conclusion 213

Credits and References 214

Appendix A - Nmap Cheat Sheet 215

Appendix B - Miscellaneous Nmap Options 223

Table of Contents

Introduction 13

Conventions Used In This Book 16

Section 0: Internet Protocol Suite 17

Internet Protocol Suite History 18

How The IP Suite Works 20

Components of TCP/IP 22

Anatomy of Segments/Datagrams, Packets, and Frames 24

Common Application Protocols and Ports 27

Section 1: Installing Nmap 31

Installing Nmap on Windows 32

Installing Nmap on Linux systems 36

Compiling Nmap from Source for Unix and Linux 37

Installing Nmap on Mac OS X 40

Section 2: Basic Scanning Techniques 45

Scan a Single Target 46

Nmap Port States 47

Understanding Port States 48

Scan Multiple Targets 50

Scan a Range of IP Addresses 51

Scan an Entire Subnet 52

CIDR Notation Reference 53

Scan a List of Targets 54

Scan Random Targets 55

Exclude Targets from a Scan 56

Exclude Targets Using a List 57

Perform an Aggressive Scan 58

Scan an IPv6 Target 59

Section 3: Discovery Options 61

Don't Ping 63

Ping Only Scan 64

TCP SYN Ping 66

TCP ACK Ping 67

UDP Ping 68

ICMP Echo Ping 69

ICMP Timestamp Ping 70

ICMP Address Mask Ping 71

IP Protocol Ping 72

ARP Ping 73

Traceroute 74

Disable Reverse DNS Resolution 75

Alternative DNS Lookup Method 76

Manually Specify DNS Server(s) 77

Create a Host List 78

Section 4: Advanced Scanning Options 79

TCP SYN Scan 80

TCP Connect Scan 81

UDP Scan 82

TCP NULL Scan 83

TCP FIN Scan 84

Xmas Scan 85

Custom TCP Scan 86

TCP ACK Scan 87

IP Protocol Scan 88

Section 5: Port Scanning Options 89

Perform a Fast Scan 90

Scan Specific Ports 91

Scan Ports by Name 92

Scan Ports by Protocol 93

Scan All Ports 94

Scan Top Ports 95

Perform a Sequential Port Scan 96

Only Display Open Ports 97

Section 6: Operating System and Service Detection 99

Operating System Detection 100

Submitting TCP/IP Fingerprints 101

Attempt to Guess an Unknown Operating System 102

Service Version Detection 103

Troubleshooting Version Scans 104

Section 7: Timing Options 107

Timing Parameters 109

Timing Templates 110

Minimum Number of Parallel Operations 111

Maximum Number of Parallel Operations 112

Minimum Host Group Size 113

Maximum Host Group Size 114

Initial RTT Timeout 115

Maximum RTT Timeout 116

Maximum Retries 117

Set the Packet TTL 118

Host Timeout 119

Minimum Scan Delay 120

Maximum Scan Delay 121

Minimum Packet Rate 122

Maximum Packet Rate 123

Defeat Reset Rate Limits 124

Section 8: Evading Firewalls 125

Fragment Packets 126

Specify a Specific MTU 127

Use a Decoy 128

9

Idle Zombie Scan 129

Manually Specify a Source Port Number.. 130

Append Random Data 131

Randomize Target Scan Order 132

Spoof MAC Address 133

Send Bad Checksums 134

Section 9: Output Options 135

Save Output to a Text File 136

Save Output to a XML File 137

Grepable Output 138

Output All Supported File Types 139

133t Output 140

Section 10: Troubleshooting and Debugging................................... 141

Getting Help 142

Display Nmap Version 143

Verbose Output 144

Debugging 145

Display Port State Reason Codes 146

Trace Packets 147

Display Host Networking Configuration 148

Specify Which Network Interface to Use 149

Section 11: Zenmap... 151

Launching Zenmap... 152

Basic Zenmap Operations 153

Zenmap Results... 154

Scanning Profiles 155

Profile Editor... 156

Viewing Open Ports 157

Viewing a Network Map.. 158

Saving Network Maps.. 159

Viewing Host Details 160

Viewing Scan History 161

Comparing Scan Results 162

Saving Scans 163

Section 12: Nmap Scripting Engine (NSE) 165

Execute Individual Scripts 166

Common Scripts 167

Execute Multiple Scripts 168

Execute Scripts by Category 169

Script Categories 170

Execute Multiple Script Categories 171

Show Script Help Files 172

Troubleshoot Scripts 173

Update the Script Database 174

Section 13: Ndiff 175

Scan Comparison Using Ndiff 176

Ndiff Verbose Mode 177

XML Output Mode 178

Section 14: Nping 179

Perform a Simple Ping 180

Hide Sent Packets 181

Hide All Packets 182

Specify A Ping Count 183

Ping Multiple Targets 184

Specify a Ping Rate 185

Specify a Ping Delay 187

Generate a Payload 188

Ping Using TCP or UDP 189

Ping Specific Ports (TCP or UDP) 191

Perform an ARP Ping 192

11

Miscellaneous Nping Options 194

Section 15: Ncat 195

    Test a Webserver 196

    Test a SMTP Server 197

    Transfer a File 198

    Create an Ad Hoc Chat Server 199

    Create an Ad Hoc Webserver 200

Section 16: Tips and Tricks 203

    Combine Multiple Options 204

    Display Scan Status 205

    Runtime Interaction 206

    Remotely Scan Your Network 208

    Scanme.Nmap.org 209

    Wireshark 210

    Nmap Online Resources 211

Conclusion 213

Credits and References 214

Appendix A - Nmap Cheat Sheet 215

Appendix B - Miscellaneous Nmap Options 223

Introduction

Nmap is a network scanning utility created by Gordon "Fyodor" Lyon that can be used to discover, audit, and troubleshoot networked systems. It is free software released under the GNU General Public License (see gnu.org/copyleft/gpl.html). Nmap is is actively developed by a community of volunteers and is an evaluable tool for network administrators and security auditors.

```
# nmap 192.168.1.1

Starting Nmap 6.47 ( http://nmap.org ) at 2015-01-31 21:52 CST
Nmap scan report for 192.168.1.1
Host is up (0.00082s latency).
Not shown: 994 closed ports
PORT      STATE SERVICE
53/tcp    open  domain
139/tcp   open  netbios-ssn
445/tcp   open  microsoft-ds
548/tcp   open  afp
5009/tcp  open  airport-admin
10000/tcp open  snet-sensor-mgmt
MAC Address: 6C:70:9F:D6:2D:94 (Apple)

Nmap done: 1 IP address (1 host up) scanned in 12.43 seconds
#
```

A typical Nmap scan

Nmap's award-winning suite of network scanning utilities have been in constant development since 1997 and continually improve with each new release. Version 6 of Nmap (released in May of 2012) adds many new features and enhancements. Some of the best new features added to Nmap 6 are listed below:

- Improved service and operating system version detection
- Better support for Windows and Mac OS X
- Addition of the Nping utility (discussed in Section 14)
- Continued enhancement of NSE (the Nmap Scripting Engine, discussed in Section 15)
- Full support for IPv6
- Better overall performance

The Nmap project relies on volunteers to support and develop this amazing tool. If you would like to help improve Nmap, there are several ways to get involved:

Promote Nmap

Nmap isn't just a tool made exclusively for "hackers". It's a wonderful program that every network administrator should know about. Despite its fame (Nmap has been featured in several movies), it isn't widely known outside of technically elite circles. You can help promote Nmap by introducing this wonderful tool to your friends or writing a blog entry about it.

Note: *Show your friends how cool Nmap is by pointing them to Nmap's movie credit page at nmap.org/movies.*

Report Bugs

You can help improve Nmap by reporting any bugs you discover to the Nmap developers. The Nmap project provides a mailing list for this, which can be found online at seclists.org/nmap-dev.

Note: *Thousands of people worldwide use Nmap. Additionally, Nmap developers are very busy people. Before reporting a bug or asking for assistance, you should search the Nmap website and mailing lists to make sure your problem hasn't already been reported or resolved.*

Contribute Code

If you're a programmer with some spare time on your hands, you can get involved with Nmap development. To learn more about contributing code to the Nmap project visit nmap.org/data/HACKING. Nmap also sponsors Google Summer of Code. If you're a student you can apply to join this annual program at nmap.org/soc and gain valuable experience while also helping to improve the Nmap suite.

Submit TCP/IP Fingerprints

If you're not a programmer, you can still improve Nmap by submitting any unknown TCP/IP fingerprints you discover while scanning. Submitting fingerprints is easy and it helps improve Nmap's software version and operating system detection capabilities. Visit nmap.org/submit/ for more information or to submit your discoveries.

Note: *More information on this topic is covered in Section 6.*

Sponsor Nmap

The Nmap project does not accept donations. If, however, you have a security related service you would like promote, you can sponsor Nmap by purchasing an advertising package on the insecure.org website. For more information, visit insecure.org/advertising.html.

Conventions Used In This Book

Nmap running on Microsoft Windows systems:

```
C:\> nmap scanme.nmap.org
```

Nmap running on non-privileged accounts for Unix/Linux/Mac OS X:

```
$ nmap scanme.nmap.org
```

Nmap running on Unix/Linux/Mac OS X systems as the root user:

```
# nmap scanme.nmap.org
```

Using the sudo command to elevate privileges for Unix/Linux/Mac OS X:

```
$ sudo nmap scanme.nmap.org
```

Note: Windows users may omit the sudo command where used in examples as its use is not necessary and will not work on Microsoft based systems.

Using command line options with Nmap:

```
# nmap -T2 scanme.nmap.org
```

Important: Nmap's command line options are case sensitive. The -T2 option (discussed in Section 7) in the example above is not the same as -t2 and will result in an error if specified in the incorrect case.

Additional Nmap output truncated (to save space):

```
[...]
```

Keyboard sequences:

```
<ENTER>, <CTRL + C>, etc.
```

16

Section 0: Internet Protocol Suite

Overview

Before you can begin working with Nmap, you must have a basic grasp of how the Internet Protocol Suite (TCP, UDP, IP, etc.) works. This section provides a high level overview of the IP Suite for beginners. True to the "Fat-Free" style, this is by no means an exhaustive guide to TCP/IP, but rather a foundation to build on. The goal is to jumpstart your understanding so that you can use Nmap effectively.

Internet Protocol Suite History

The Internet Protocol Suite is a set of communication protocols that drive modern networks and the Internet. The IP Suite is often referred to as TCP/IP, short for Transmission Control Protocol/Internet Protocol, which are two of the core protocols defined in the IP Suite. Beyond TCP and IP, there are many other protocols that make up the complete IP Suite including ARP (Address Resolution Protocol), DNS (Domain Name System), DHCP (Dynamic Host Configuration Protocol), and dozens more.

The Internet Protocol Suite is the brilliant result of a United States Department of Defense project dating back to the 1960's. The seeds for TCP/IP were planted with the creation of DoD's ARPANET, a precursor to the Internet. The goal of ARPANET (short for Advanced Research Projects Agency Network) was to create a reliable network so researchers across the country could share computing power – which was hard to come by at the time. The solution was a "packet switched" network that could connect numerous systems to a large network backbone.

Packet switched networks break data down into tiny units of information (packets) and then relay them to the desired destination. It is a framework designed to allow bidirectional communication with multiple systems simultaneously. This is something we take for granted today in an era where everyone has the Internet in their pocket; however, before ARPANET a framework for multi-host shared network communication didn't exist.

The ARPANET packet switching system proved to be a successful framework for networking, but as it grew fundamental flaws were found with its original design. While the core packet switching technology worked brilliantly, the initial communication protocols developed for ARPANET didn't scale well. To remedy this, researchers decided to build an improved set of communication protocols to run on packet switched networks that would help the ARPANET grow and be more reliable. The solution was the Internet Protocol Suite.

The IP Suite was developed as a platform independent set of networking standards that run on top of packet switched networks. The primary goal of the IP Suite was to be more flexible than earlier communications protocols. It also shifted the responsibility of data integrity from the network itself to the hosts, which helped improve scalability of the packet switching system.

Throughout the 1970's, TCP/IP was developed/refined and four different versions were created. The final version, known as TCP/IP v4, was ratified in 1981 and by the early 1990's it had been adopted by most computing platforms. The advent of the World Wide Web combined with the power of TCP/IP and packet switched networks lead to the digital revolution that touches nearly every aspect of our lives today.

The creators of IPv4 thought of nearly everything. Reliability, scalability, and interoperability were all built into the standard. One thing they didn't plan for, however, was the need for more than the 4.3-billion IP addresses that IPv4 provides. IPv6 solves this by increasing the address space to 2^{128}. That number in human readable form is:

340,282,366,920,938,463,463,374,607,431,768,211,456

To try to visualize a number that large, just imagine that IPv6 provides for the ability to assign about 4-quadrillion IP addresses to every star in the known universe. While IPv4 is still the dominant version, IPv6 is slowly emerging as its successor.

Note: *Wondering what happened to IPv5? The short answer is that there is no IPv5. The Internet Protocol number 5 was assigned to an experimental streaming protocol, but it was not a successor to IPv4 and was never known as IPv5.*

How The IP Suite Works

TCP/IP provides an elegant method of networking various systems together. The core architecture is defined as the TCP/IP Model. The TCP/IP Model divides the IP Suite into four layers and assigns various functions to each layer. This simplifies the protocol and contributes to its robustness. The table below provides an overview of the TCP/IP model layers and common protocols associated with each layer.

Layer	Common Protocols	Devices
Application Layer	DNS, DHCP, HTTP, FTP, SMTP, IMAP, POP, SSH	
Transport Layer	TCP, UDP	
Internet Layer	IPv4, IPv6, ICMP, IGMP	Routers
Link Layer	MAC (Ethernet), ARP, PPP, L2TP	Network interfaces, cables, switches

TCP/IP Model and common protocols

The **Application Layer** is where programs run. On a host system, applications are given access to the operating system's TCP/IP stack. When an application such as a web browser needs to communicate with the network, it hands the request to the system's TCP/IP stack. Then, it is pushed down the layers on the sending side and back up the layers on the receiving side. This frees the application from having to know how to directly communicate with the remote system because the lower layers handle all of the connectivity.

The **Transport Layer** establishes communication between two hosts. This is done using a transport protocol such as TCP (Transmission Control Protocol) or UDP (User Datagram Protocol). The protocols on this layer are responsible for the reliability, or lack thereof, of the communication channel.

The **Internet Layer** is where addressing and routing are handled. This is the layer where the Internet exists. Routers facilitate the flow of data from the source network to the destination network using an IP address. Firewalls may also be involved at this layer to provide security and translation from public to private addresses.

The **Link Layer** is the physical connection to the network. The link layer consists of the host's network interface along with a connection medium of some sort (typically a cable). The link provides a connection to other hosts on the local network. This is usually a switch or hub but can also be "thin air" when linking via a wireless network.

An alternative to the TCP/IP model is the OSI 7 layer model. This model was developed independently and is compatible with the TCP/IP model – although it is stricter in comparison – while still being compatible with the original framework. The following table illustrates the differences between the two models.

TCP/IP Model	OSI Model
Application	Application
	Presentation
	Session
Transport	Transport
Network	Network
Link	Data Link
	Physical

TCP/IP Model compared to the OSI Model

The layered approach to network communication has proven to be a reliable framework for creating a massive global network of networks (otherwise known as the Internet). The concept is something that was far ahead of its time when it was developed. We should be grateful for the contributions of everyone involved. Some of the key people responsible for developing or influencing packet switching and TCP/IP are listed below.

Name	Country	Accomplishment
Donald Davies	United Kingdom	Inventors of packet switched networks
Paul Baran	United States	
Louis Pouzin	France	Researchers who pioneered concepts that lead to the creation of TCP/IP
Hubert Zimmermann	France	
Vinton Gray Cerf	United States	Creators of TCP/IP
Robert Kahn	United States	

Networking pioneers (source: Wikipedia)

Society is indebted to these brilliant scientists, researchers, and engineers, plus many other unsung heroes for their contributions to networking.

Components of TCP/IP

Now that we have covered the history and fundamental architecture of the TCP/IP model, it's time to dive into the key elements that make it work. The list below provides an overview of the core components of TCP/IP.

IP Addresses: A numerical (IPv4) or hexadecimal (IPv6) address assigned to a network device. The IP address identifies the system it is assigned to and allows it to be located on a local or wide area network.

Ports: A port is a numerical address assigned to an application or protocol on a networked system. The port number identifies the service or program running at the numbered location. There are 65,535 ports available for use. Common examples of ports are 25 for SMTP, 53 for DNS, and 80 for HTTP.

Note: *More common port numbers will be discussed later in this chapter.*

Protocols: A protocol is the defined syntax for communication between networked systems. Protocols operate at various levels of the TCP/IP model and when layered together allow dissimilar systems to speak a common language and communicate effectively. Common examples are TCP, UDP, HTTP, SMTP, and DNS.

Segments: A segment (also known as a datagram) is the first stage of dividing up data for transmission on a packet switched network. Segments are generated at the Transport layer of the TCP/IP and OSI (layer 4) models. The most common examples of transport layer protocols are TCP and UDP.

Packets: Packets are units of data that are transmitted and received on a network. A packet is the form of data used at the Internet layer of the TCP/IP model or the Network Layer (Layer 3) of the OSI model. Segments are turned into packets in preparation for transmission over a link.

Frames: A frame is the next unit of data below a packet. Packets are converted into frames as they are transmitted across a physical network connection. The frame itself is a collection of bits (discussed next).

Bits: Bits are the "ones and zeroes" of computing. Bits are binary values that are a digital representation of the data being transmitted electrically across a network link/interface.

These concepts combine to make up the core of modern networking systems. Applications use IP addresses to reference each other. Ports are established between IP addresses for utilizing protocols. Segments/datagrams are created from application data and turned into packets. Then, network interfaces turn packets into frames and bits. This process of layering protocols is known as *encapsulation*.

Information flows up and down the TCP/IP stack on each side of the connection at impressive rates. This cycle repeats many hundreds (or thousands) of times per second. The result is a marvel of engineering that allows computers to talk to each other.

Anatomy of Segments/Datagrams, Packets, and Frames

It's fascinating to think about how information flows across packet switched networks. Everything is beautifully orchestrated using a collection of protocols. Data is broken down into tiny chunks, transmitted across a connection, and then reassembled on the receiving side. This is the miracle that allows us to watch cat videos online whenever we please.

When it comes to Nmap, IP packets and TCP/UDP segments and datagrams are the keys to how the scanner works its magic. The information gleaned from analyzing this data allows Nmap to determine if ports on a target system are open or closed. The incredibly clever Nmap developers have also figured out how to use this information to determine which application versions and underlying operating system are running on the target system. This makes Nmap a great tool for network analysis.

Since these components are central to how Nmap works, let's delve a little deeper to understand how they are structured so we can better understand the program's features.

TCP Segments and UDP Datagrams

TCP and UDP are the two most common transport protocols. TCP uses a robust packet structure to provide reliable delivery of data between hosts on a network. In contrast, UDP is a simpler protocol that is less reliable, but in turn requires less processing overhead. Packets for both protocols consist of a header along with payload data. The diagrams below illustrate the structure of each protocol's PDU (Protocol Data Unit).

Source Port			Destination Port	
Sequence Number				
Acknowledgment Number				
Data Offset	Reserved	Flags	Windows Size	
Checksum			Urgent Pointer	
Options				
Data				

TCP segment PDU

Information in the TCP header is utilized to route the data stream to the proper port location in a reliable and ordered fashion. TCP uses sequences, acknowledgments, and windows to ensure proper delivery of data to the target system. This structure is what makes TCP considered a reliable "connection-oriented" transport protocol.

The information in the UDP header is much simpler. UDP does not provide guaranteed delivery, so less information is required in the datagram. This reduces overhead and latency at the expense of reliability, which makes UDP considered a "connectionless" transport protocol.

Source Port	Destination Port
Length	Checksum
Data	

UDP datagram PDU

IP Packets

PDUs for TCP/UDP are encapsulated in IP packets for transmission on packet switched networks. The IP packet consists of a header and the TCP or UDP payload data. The following diagram describes the IP packet structure.

Version	IHL	DSCP	ECN	Total Length	
Identification				Flags	Fragment Offset
Time To Live		Protocol		Header Checksum	
Source Address					
Destination Address					
Options					
Data					

IP packet

The IP protocol analyzes the header in each packet to determine where it needs to be relayed to reach its final destination. Each IP packet header contains information about the source/destination addresses, type of protocol being used, packet size, and a number of optional flags. There are also a number of other fields that help ensure timely and reliable delivery to the destination address such the checksum and TTL.

Ethernet Frames

When a packet is ready to be transmitted, it is converted into an Ethernet frame. The frame encapsulates the packet in a simple structure that has a header with addressing and signaling information plus a trailer that is used for error checking. The diagram below describes the ethernet frame structure.

Preamble	Start Frame Delimiter	Destination MAC Address	Source MAC Address	VLAN Tag	Length	Data	Frame Check Sequence

Ethernet frame structure

Putting It All Together

When you stack everything together you get a nice sandwich of protocols that dictate how data flows across a network connection. The information in the protocol headers is utilized to facilitate the communication exchange at each step along the way. The result is reliable communication between hosts on a network.

Ethernet Frame Header
IP Packet Header
TCP/UDP Header
Data
Ethernet Frame Trailer

Encapsulation of network PDUs

The information in the protocol headers is the nuts and bolts that make TCP/IP function. Later in this guide, you will learn how Nmap can be used to control the fields in these headers when scanning. This will allow you to generate custom probes in an attempt to generate a response from a target system.

Common Application Protocols and Ports

TCP and UDP make use of 65,535 ports for network communication. Of these, only a handful are commonly used for hosting network application services. The list below describes some of the most well-known services along with their associated port numbers and transport protocols.

20 TCP
FTP Data

21 TCP
FTP Control

22 TCP|UDP
Secure Shell (SSH)

23 TCP
Telnet

25 TCP
Simple Mail Transfer Protocol (SMTP)

42 TCP|UDP
Windows Internet Name Service (WINS)

53 TCP|UDP
Domain Name System (DNS)

67 UDP
DHCP Server

68 UDP
DHCP Client

69 UDP
Trivial File Transfer Protocol (TFTP)

80 TCP|UDP
Hypertext Transfer Protocol (HTTP)

110 TCP
Post Office Protocol 3 (POP3)

119 TCP
Network News Transfer Protocol (NNTP)

123 UDP
Network Time Protocol (NTP)

135 TCP|UDP
Microsoft RPC

137 TCP|UDP
NetBIOS Name Service

138 TCP|UDP
NetBIOS Datagram Service

139 TCP|UDP
NetBIOS Session Service

143 TCP|UDP
Internet Message Access Protocol (IMAP)

161 TCP|UDP
Simple Network Management Protocol (SNMP)

162 TCP|UDP
Simple Network Management Protocol (SNMP) Trap

389 TCP|UDP
Lightweight Directory Access Protocol (LDAP)

443 TCP|UDP
Hypertext Transfer Protocol over TLS/SSL (HTTPS)

445 TCP
Server Message Block (SMB)

636 TCP|UDP
Lightweight Directory Access Protocol over TLS/SSL (LDAPS)

873 TCP
Remote File Synchronization Protocol (RSYNC)

993 TCP
Internet Message Access Protocol over SSL (IMAPS)

995 TCP
Post Office Protocol 3 over TLS/SSL (POP3S)

1433 TCP
Microsoft SQL Server Database

3306 TCP
MySQL Database

3389 TCP

Microsoft Terminal Server/Remote Desktop Protocol (RDP)

5800 TCP

Virtual Network Computing (VNC) web interface

5900 TCP

Virtual Network Computing (VNC) remote desktop

This is just a short list of some of the most common port numbers used on modern networks. Ports 0 through 1023 are reserved for "well-known services". These ports are central to common services associated with basic network functionality. Ports 1024 through 49151 are registered with the Internet Assigned Numbers Authority for use with vendor specific network based applications. Ports 49152 to 65535 are dynamic ports that are primarily used for outbound connections from client systems.

Tip: See *wikipedia.org/wiki/List_of_TCP_and_UDP_port_numbers* for a longer list of notable ports and their associated usage.

Section 1: Installing Nmap

Overview

Installing Nmap is a simple process similar to installing just about any other software package. Nmap has its roots in the Linux world, but Windows and Mac OS X versions are also available for easy installation. Additionally, Nmap can run on many Unix platforms like Solaris or BSD.

While great care is taken to make Nmap a universal experience on every platform, the reality is that you may experience "issues" when using Nmap on Windows, Unix, or Mac OS X. This is primarily because these platforms have various idiosyncrasies that are not present on a typical Linux system.

Linux is the ideal platform for running Nmap because of its robust networking stack. Recent releases of Nmap, however, have greatly improved compatibility on alternative operating systems like Windows and Mac OS X. Running Nmap version 5 or newer on these systems is much more reliable compared to older releases. Nmap 6 continues this trend of making Windows and Mac OS X "first class citizens" by continuing to resolve platform specific problems.

Topics covered in this Section:

- Installing Nmap on Windows
- Installing Nmap on Linux
- Installing Nmap from source (Unix and Linux)
- Installing Nmap on Mac OS X

Installing Nmap on Windows

Step 1

Download the Windows version of Nmap from nmap.org.

Step 2

Launch the Nmap setup program. Select the default installation (recommended), which will install the entire Nmap suite of utilities.

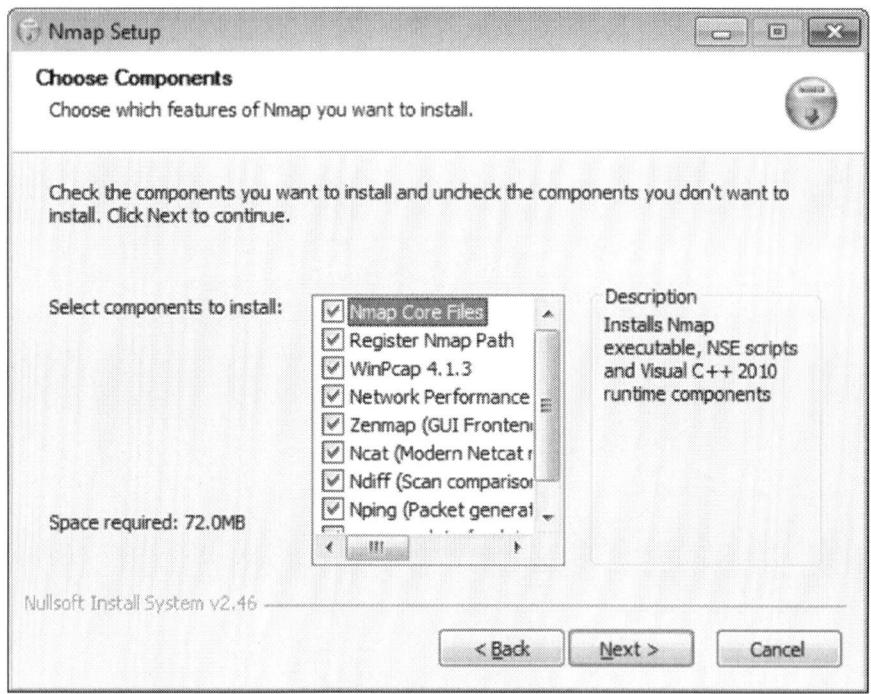

Nmap for Windows installer

Step 3

During installation, a helper program called WinPcap will also be installed. WinPcap is required for Nmap to function properly on the Windows platform so do not skip this step.

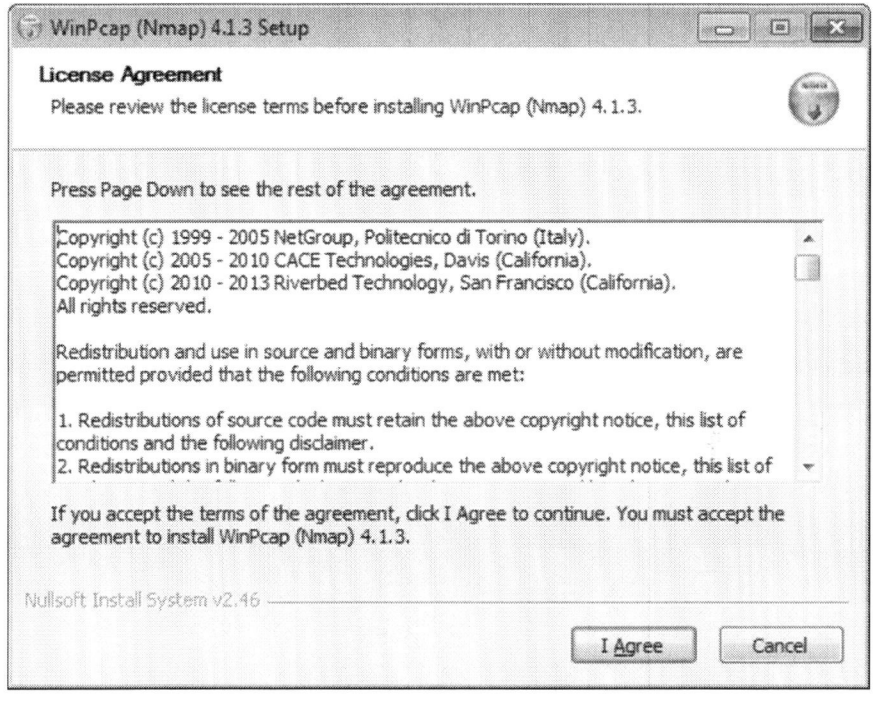

WinPcap for Windows installer

Step 4

After the WinPcap installation has completed, you are given the option to configure its service settings. The default options will enable the WinPcap service to start when Windows boots. This is recommended as Nmap will not function correctly when the WinPcap service is not running.

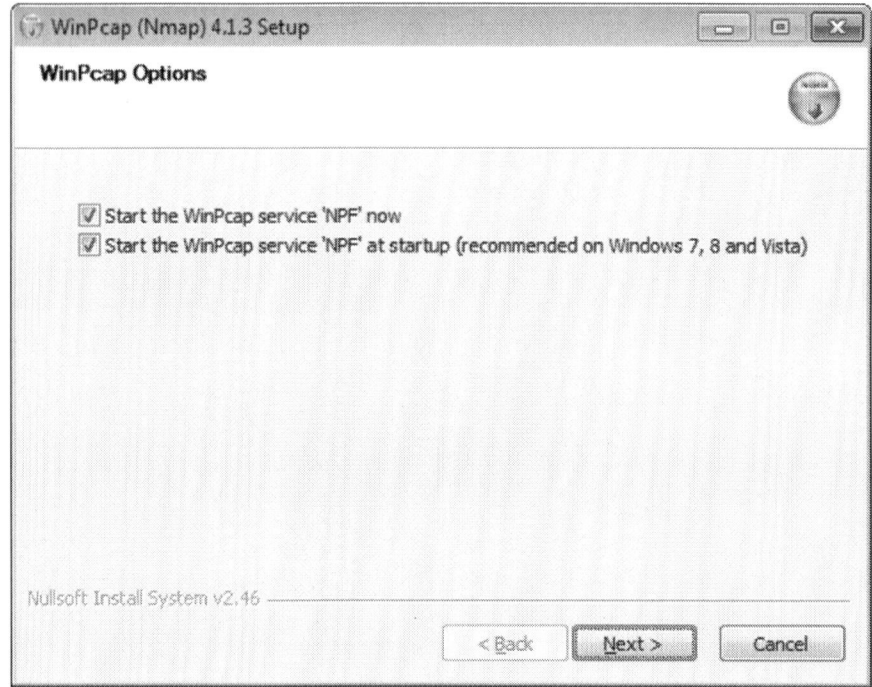

WinPcap options

Step 5

Once Nmap has been successfully installed you can verify it is working correctly by executing **nmap scanme.nmap.org** on the command line (located in Start > Programs > Accessories > Command Prompt).

```
C:\> nmap scanme.nmap.org

Starting Nmap 6.47 ( http://nmap.org ) at 2015-01-16 08:09 CST
Nmap scan report for scanme.nmap.org (74.207.244.221)
Host is up (0.058s latency).
Not shown: 997 closed ports
PORT      STATE SERVICE
22/tcp    open  ssh
80/tcp    open  http
9929/tcp  open  nping-echo

Nmap done: 1 IP address (1 host up) scanned in 1.16 seconds
```

Nmap test scan on Microsoft Windows

If the results of your scan are similar to the results above, then you have successfully installed Nmap. If you receive an error, refer to Section 10 of this book for troubleshooting and debugging information.

Tip: Consider using the Power Shell for Windows to run Nmap. It allows for flexible windows resizing to better accommodate Nmap's output. This can be found in Start > Programs > Accessories > Windows PowerShell > PowerShell on Windows 7 based systems.

Installing Nmap on Linux systems

Most popular Linux distributions provide binary Nmap packages, which allows for simple installation. Installation on Unix systems typically requires compiling Nmap from source code (as described next in this section).

Note: The sudo command is used to elevate privileges on Linux systems. This is the default behavior for most modern systems. If you are logged in as the root user you can omit the sudo command.

Installing Precompiled Packages for Linux

For Debian and Ubuntu based systems:

```
$ sudo apt-get install nmap
```

For Red Hat and Fedora based systems:

```
$ sudo yum install nmap
```

The version of Nmap found in the software repositories for your Linux distribution may not be the most recent version available. You can check to see which version of Nmap you have installed by executing **nmap -V** (capital V) as demonstrated below.

```
$ nmap -V

Nmap version 6.47 ( http://nmap.org )
Platform: x86_64-pc-linux-gnu
Compiled with: liblua-5.2.3 openssl-1.0.1f libpcre-8.31 libpcap-1.5.3 nmap-libdnet-1.12 ipv6
Compiled without:
Available nsock engines: epoll poll select
```

Nmap version output

Compare the version that is installed with the most recent version available on the nmap.org website. If the release is too far out of date, you may want to consider downloading the source code for Nmap and compiling a newer version for your system. Instructions for doing this are discussed next.

Compiling Nmap from Source for Unix and Linux

Another method for installing Nmap is to download and compile the source code from the nmap.org website. Building Nmap from source takes a little extra work, but is well worth the effort to get the new features and fixes in Nmap's latest releases. The following five steps detail the procedure for installing Nmap from source.

Step 1

Download the Nmap 6 source from nmap.org/download.html. This can be done via a standard web browser or from the command line using the **wget** command found on most Unix/Linux based systems.

```
$ wget http://nmap.org/dist/nmap-6.47.tgz
--2015-01-13 19:00:02--  http://nmap.org/dist/nmap-6.47.tgz
Resolving nmap.org (nmap.org)... 173.255.243.189,
2600:3c01::f03c:91ff:fe70:d085
Connecting to nmap.org (nmap.org)|173.255.243.189|:80... connected.
HTTP request sent, awaiting response... 200 OK
Length: 9796783 (9.3M) [application/x-tar]
Saving to: 'nmap-6.47.tgz'

100%[===========================>] 9,796,783    1.99MB/s    in 4.5s

2015-01-13 19:00:07 (2.06 MB/s) - 'nmap-6.47.tgz' saved
[9796783/9796783]
```

Downloading Nmap on Unix and Linux systems via the command line

Step 2

Extract the contents of the Nmap package by executing the **tar** command.

```
$ tar -xvf nmap-6.47.tgz
[...]
```

Extracting Nmap source code

Step 3

Configure and build the Nmap source code by changing to the source directory and then executing **./configure && make** on the command line.

```
$ cd nmap-6.47/
$ ./configure && make
checking build system type... x86_64-unknown-linux-gnu
checking host system type... x86_64-unknown-linux-gnu
checking for gcc... gcc
checking for C compiler default output file name... a.out
checking whether the C compiler works... yes
[...]
```

Compiling Nmap source code

Step 4

Install the compiled code by typing **sudo make install** on the command line.

Note: This step will require root privileges. You must login as the root user or use the **sudo** command to complete this step.

```
$ sudo make install
Password: ********
/usr/bin/install -c -d /usr/local/bin /usr/local/share/man/man1
/usr/local/share/nmap
/usr/bin/install -c -c -m 755 nmap /usr/local/bin/nmap
/usr/bin/strip -x /usr/local/bin/nmap
/usr/bin/install -c -c -m 644 docs/nmap.1 /usr/local/share/man/man1/
/usr/bin/install -c -c -m 644 docs/nmap.xsl /usr/local/share/nmap/
[...]
NMAP SUCCESSFULLY INSTALLED
```

Installing Nmap from source code

Step 5

Once Nmap has been successfully installed, you can verify it is working correctly by executing **nmap scanme.nmap.org** on the command line.

```
$ nmap scanme.nmap.org

Starting Nmap 6.47 ( http://nmap.org ) at 2015-01-16 08:20 CST
Nmap scan report for scanme.nmap.org (74.207.244.221)
Host is up (0.059s latency).
Not shown: 997 closed ports
PORT      STATE SERVICE
22/tcp    open  ssh
80/tcp    open  http
9929/tcp  open  nping-echo

Nmap done: 1 IP address (1 host up) scanned in 2.62 seconds
```

Nmap test scan on Unix/Linux

If the results of your scan are similar to the results above, then you have successfully installed Nmap. If you receive an error, refer to Section 10 of this book for troubleshooting and debugging information.

Installing Nmap on Mac OS X

Step 1

Download the Mac OS X version of Nmap from nmap.org.

Note: *Nmap 5 is the last release to support running on PowerPC based systems. Version 6 and newer runs exclusively on Mac systems with Intel processors.*

Step 2

Launch the Nmap setup program and click continue. Then, accept the license terms of the Nmap program.

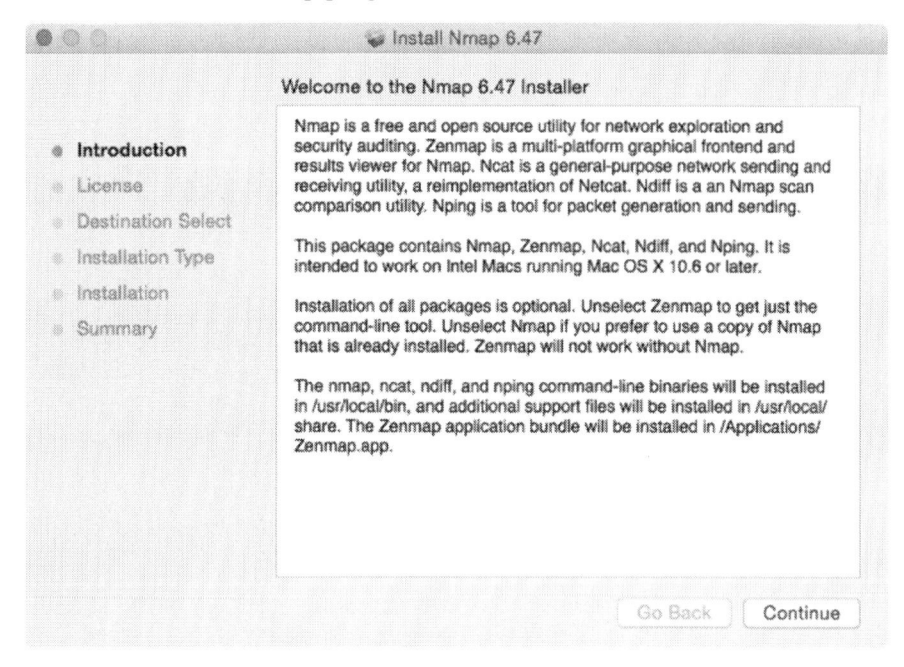

Nmap for Mac OS X installer

Step 3

When prompted for the installation options, leave the default selections checked (recommended) and click continue to begin the install process. This will install the entire Nmap suite of utilities.

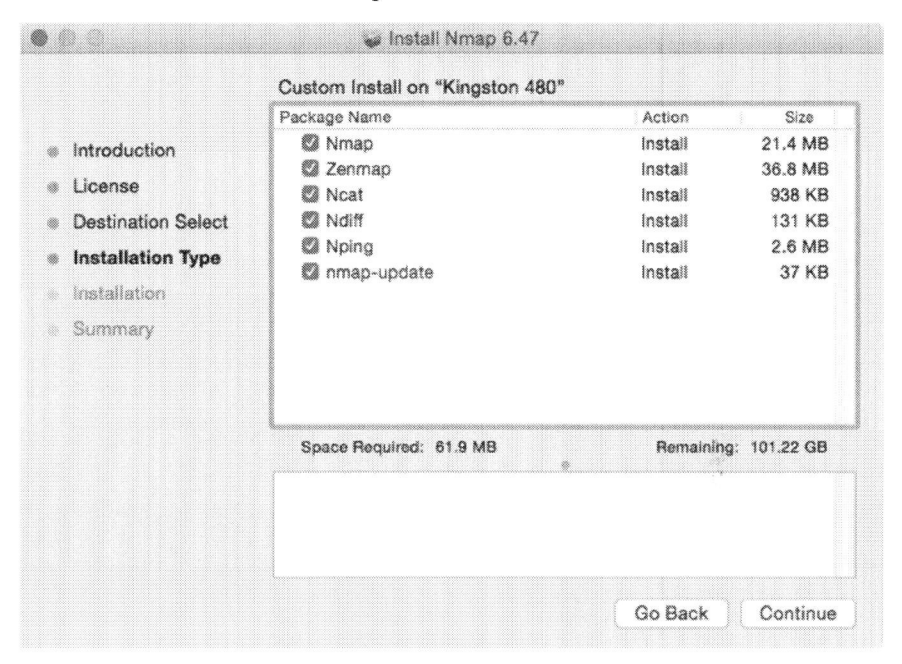

Default installation settings

Step 4

Follow the prompts and enter your administrative password if required. When the installation is complete you can close the Nmap installer.

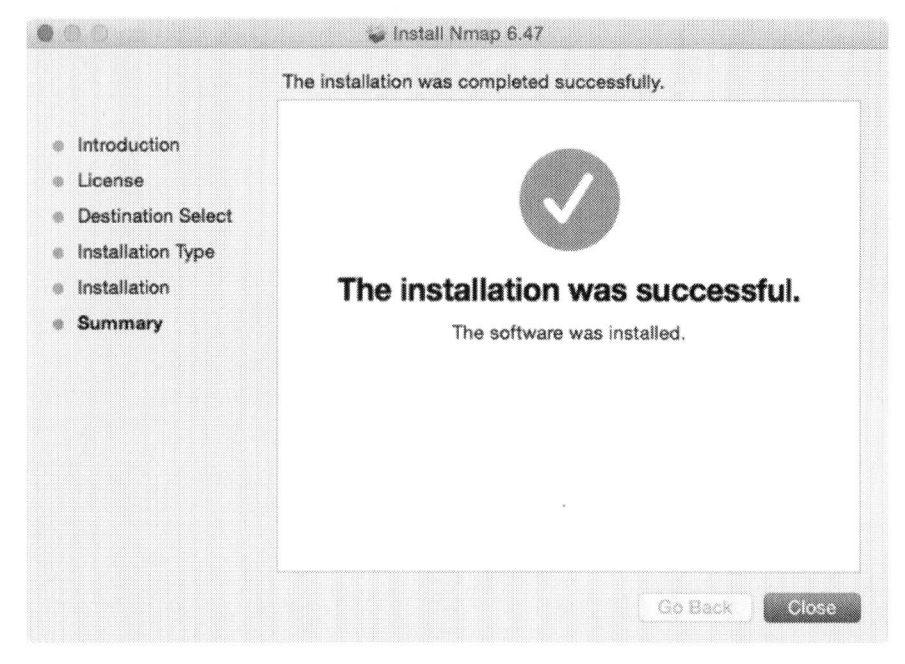

Successful installation of Nmap on Mac OS X

Step 5

Once Nmap has been successfully installed, you can verify it is working correctly by executing **nmap scanme.nmap.org** in the Mac OS X Terminal application (located in Applications > Utilities > Terminal).

```
$ nmap scanme.nmap.org

Starting Nmap 6.47 ( http://nmap.org ) at 2015-01-15 20:05 CST
Nmap scan report for scanme.nmap.org (74.207.244.221)
Host is up (0.082s latency).
Not shown: 997 closed ports
PORT      STATE SERVICE
22/tcp    open  ssh
80/tcp    open  http
9929/tcp  open  nping-echo

Nmap done: 1 IP address (1 host up) scanned in 2.43 seconds
```

Nmap test scan on Mac OS X

If the results of your scan are similar to the results above, then you have successfully installed Nmap. If you receive an error, refer to Section 10 of this book for troubleshooting and debugging information.

Section 2: Basic Scanning Techniques

Overview

This section covers the basics of network scanning with Nmap. Before we begin it is important to understand the following concepts:

- Firewalls, routers, proxy servers, and other security devices can skew the results of an Nmap scan. Because of this, scanning remote hosts that are not on your local network may produce misleading information.

- Some scanning options require elevated privileges. On Unix and Linux systems you may be required to login as the root user or to execute Nmap using the sudo command.

There are also a couple of warnings to take into consideration:

- Scanning networks that you do not have permission to scan can get you in trouble with your internet service provider, the police, and possibly even the government. Don't scan the FBI or Secret Service websites unless you want to get in trouble.

- Aggressively scanning some systems can lead to undesirable results such as system downtime and or loss. Always scan mission critical systems with caution.

Now let's start scanning!

Scan a Single Target

Executing Nmap with no command line options will perform a basic scan on the target system. A target can be specified as an IP address or host name (which Nmap will try to resolve).

Usage syntax: nmap [target]

```
$ nmap 192.168.1.1

Starting Nmap 6.47 ( http://nmap.org ) at 2015-01-13 19:23 CST
Nmap scan report for 192.168.1.1
Host is up (0.00084s latency).
Not shown: 994 closed ports
PORT       STATE SERVICE
53/tcp     open  domain
139/tcp    open  netbios-ssn
445/tcp    open  microsoft-ds
548/tcp    open  afp
5009/tcp   open  airport-admin
10000/tcp  open  snet-sensor-mgmt

Nmap done: 1 IP address (1 host up) scanned in 12.32 seconds
```

Single target scan

The resulting scan shows the status of ports detected on the specified target along with other helpful information such as the protocol in use and service associated with the port. The table below describes the output fields displayed by the scan.

PORT
Port number/protocol

STATE
Status of the port

SERVICE
Type of service associated with the port

A default Nmap scan will check for the 1000 most commonly used TCP/IP ports. Ports that respond to a probe are classified into one of six port states: open, closed, filtered, unfiltered, open|filtered, closed|filtered. Descriptions of these port states are described on the following page.

Nmap Port States

Nmap uses six different port states to classify the status of a port scan. The list below describes the meaning of each port state.

open

An open port is a port that actively responds to an incoming connection.

closed

A closed port is a port on a target that actively responds to a probe but does not appear to have any service running on the port. Closed ports are commonly found on systems where no firewall is in place to filter incoming traffic.

filtered

Filtered ports are ports that are typically protected by a firewall of some sort that prevents Nmap from determining whether the port is open or closed.

unfiltered

An unfiltered port is a port that Nmap can access but is unable to determine whether it is open or closed.

open|filtered

An open|filtered port is a port which Nmap believes to be open or filtered but cannot definitively determine which state the port is actually in.

closed|filtered

A closed|filtered port is a port that Nmap believes to be closed or filtered but cannot definitively determine which state the port is actually in.

Understanding Port States

Take a look at the following scan...

```
# nmap scanme.nmap.org

Starting Nmap 6.47 ( http://nmap.org ) at 2015-01-17 11:51 CST
Nmap scan report for scanme.nmap.org (74.207.244.221)
Host is up, received reset (0.30s latency).
Not shown: 997 closed ports
Reason: 997 resets
PORT       STATE SERVICE
22/tcp     open  ssh
80/tcp     open  http
9929/tcp   open  nping-echo

Nmap done: 1 IP address (1 host up) scanned in 3.08 seconds
```

Nmap scan from a dedicated internet connection

This scan shows the results of scanning a remote target from a dedicated commercial internet connection. Now review the following scan on the same target, which was performed using a consumer broadband connection.

```
# nmap scanme.nmap.org

Starting Nmap 6.47 ( http://nmap.org ) at 2015-01-17 19:21 CST
Nmap scan report for scanme.nmap.org (74.207.244.221)
Host is up, received echo-reply (0.087s latency).
Not shown: 990 closed ports
Reason: 990 resets
PORT       STATE     SERVICE
21/tcp     open      ftp
22/tcp     open      ssh
25/tcp     filtered  smtp
80/tcp     open      http
135/tcp    filtered  msrpc
139/tcp    filtered  netbios-ssn
445/tcp    filtered  microsoft-ds
554/tcp    open      rtsp
7070/tcp   open      realserver
9929/tcp   open      nping-echo

Nmap done: 1 IP address (1 host up) scanned in 5.74 seconds
```

Nmap scan from a broadband internet connection

The above scan differs from the first scan because the internet provider is performing filtering on outbound connections, whereas the first provider is not. In this case, they prevent home internet subscribers from being able to run an SMTP server and also block ports common to Microsoft Windows systems (135, 139, 445) that can be exploited by viruses. Additionally, a consumer brand router on the broadband connection is intercepting traffic destined for ports 21, 554, and 7070 and actively responds to them as it attempts to proxy protocols on those ports. In these cases, the ports are not actually open/filtered on the target system. Rather, they have been tampered with en route to the destination.

It's important to keep in mind that when scanning remote systems your results may be skewed. This can happen at any stage between you and the target. Two good rules-of-thumb when trying to interpret scan results are listed below.

"The less expensive a connection is, the more problematic it will be for scanning."

Companies providing internet service for the masses are quite likely to have traffic restrictions. You can expect home broadband connections and free Wi-Fi at Starbucks to be more susceptible to filtering than a dedicated internet connection.

"The third port state is usually a suspect."

On a typical system, you can generally expect to see a mixture of only two port states such as open/closed or open/filtered. Notice how the second scan reports ports that are open, closed, and filtered. The presence of three port states can indicate that "man-in-the-middle" filtering is taking place.

Scan Multiple Targets

Nmap can be used to scan multiple hosts at the same time. The easiest way to do this is to string together the target IP addresses or host names on the command line.

Usage syntax: nmap [target1 target2 etc]

```
$ nmap 192.168.1.1 192.168.1.109 192.168.1.155

Starting Nmap 6.47 ( http://nmap.org ) at 2015-01-13 19:30 CST
Nmap scan report for 192.168.1.1
Host is up (0.0012s latency).
Not shown: 994 closed ports
PORT       STATE SERVICE
53/tcp     open  domain
139/tcp    open  netbios-ssn
445/tcp    open  microsoft-ds
548/tcp    open  afp
5009/tcp   open  airport-admin
10000/tcp  open  snet-sensor-mgmt

Nmap scan report for 192.168.1.109
Host is up (0.00026s latency).
Not shown: 999 closed ports
PORT   STATE SERVICE
22/tcp open  ssh

Nmap done: 3 IP addresses (2 hosts up) scanned in 3.85 seconds
```

Multiple target scan

The example above demonstrates using Nmap to scan three addresses at the same time. You can use any combination of IP addresses and hostnames (separated by a space). At the end of the scan, a status line is printed with a summary of the results. In this case, only two of the three addresses responded to the probes.

Tip: *Since all three targets in the above example are on the same subnet you could use the shorthand notation of* **nmap 192.168.1.1,109,155** *to achieve the same results.*

Scan a Range of IP Addresses

Nmap can also accept a range of IP addresses for target specification.

Usage syntax: nmap [range]

```
$ nmap 192.168.1.1-100

Starting Nmap 6.47 ( http://nmap.org ) at 2015-01-13 19:32 CST
Nmap scan report for 192.168.1.1
Host is up (0.00100s latency).
Not shown: 994 closed ports
PORT       STATE SERVICE
53/tcp     open  domain
139/tcp    open  netbios-ssn
445/tcp    open  microsoft-ds
548/tcp    open  afp
5009/tcp   open  airport-admin
10000/tcp  open  snet-sensor-mgmt

Nmap scan report for 192.168.1.100
Host is up (0.0029s latency).
Not shown: 996 closed ports
PORT       STATE SERVICE
88/tcp     open  kerberos-sec
3689/tcp   open  rendezvous
5900/tcp   open  vnc
49152/tcp  open  unknown

Nmap done: 100 IP addresses (2 hosts up) scanned in 15.48 seconds
```

Scanning a range of IP addresses

In this example, Nmap is instructed to scan the range of IP addresses from 192.168.1.1 through 192.168.1.100. You can also use ranges to scan multiple networks/subnets. For example typing **nmap 192.168.1-100.*** would scan the class C IP networks of 192.168.1.1 through 192.168.100.255.

Note: *The asterisk is a wildcard character that represents all valid ranges from 0-255.*

Tip: *When scanning large ranges, use the more command with a "pipe"(i.e.* **nmap 192.168.1.1-100 | more***) to display the output one page at a time.*

Scan an Entire Subnet

Nmap can be used to scan an entire subnet using CIDR (Classless Inter-Domain Routing) notation.

Usage syntax: nmap [network/CIDR]

```
$ nmap 192.168.1.1/24 | more

Starting Nmap 6.47 ( http://nmap.org ) at 2015-01-13 19:35 CST
Nmap scan report for 192.168.1.1
Host is up (0.00081s latency).
Not shown: 994 closed ports
PORT       STATE SERVICE
53/tcp     open  domain
139/tcp    open  netbios-ssn
445/tcp    open  microsoft-ds
548/tcp    open  afp
5009/tcp   open  airport-admin
10000/tcp  open  snet-sensor-mgmt

[...]

Nmap scan report for 192.168.1.111
Host is up (0.0016s latency).
Not shown: 999 closed ports
PORT   STATE SERVICE
22/tcp open  ssh

Nmap done: 256 IP addresses (7 hosts up) scanned in 45.77 seconds
```

Scanning an entire class C subnet using CIDR notation

The above example demonstrates using Nmap to scan the entire 192.168.1.0 network using CIDR notation. CIDR notation consists of the network address and subnet mask (in binary bits) separated by a slash. In this case, /24 corresponds to a subnet mask of 255.255.255.0.

The table on the following page provides a cross-reference of CIDR notations for IPv4 networks.

CIDR Notation Reference

Classless Inter-Domain Routing notation is a shorthand method for referencing a subnet mask. The number represents the count of binary bits in the network portion of the mask. The table below shows all IPv4 subnet masks in dotted decimal notation and their CIDR notation equivalents.

Subnet Mask	CIDR
000.000.000.000	/0
128.000.000.000	/1
192.000.000.000	/2
224.000.000.000	/3
240.000.000.000	/4
248.000.000.000	/5
252.000.000.000	/6
254.000.000.000	/7
255.000.000.000	/8
255.128.000.000	/9
255.192.000.000	/10
255.224.000.000	/11
255.240.000.000	/12
255.248.000.000	/13
255.252.000.000	/14
255.254.000.000	/15
255.255.000.000	/16
255.255.128.000	/17
255.255.192.000	/18
255.255.224.000	/19
255.255.240.000	/20
255.255.248.000	/21
255.255.252.000	/22
255.255.254.000	/23
255.255.255.000	/24
255.255.255.128	/25
255.255.255.192	/26
255.255.255.224	/27
255.255.255.240	/28
255.255.255.248	/29
255.255.255.252	/30
255.255.255.254	/31
255.255.255.255	/32

Scan a List of Targets

If you have a large number of systems to scan, you can enter the IP address (or host names) in a text file and use that file as input for Nmap on the command line.

```
$ cat list.txt
192.168.1.1
192.168.1.100
192.168.1.105
```

Target IP addresses in a text file

The list.txt file above contains a list of hosts to be scanned. Each entry in the list.txt file must be separated by a space, tab, or new line. The -iL parameter is used to instruct Nmap to extract the list of targets from the list.txt file.

Usage syntax: nmap -iL [list.txt]

```
$ nmap -iL list.txt

Starting Nmap 6.47 ( http://nmap.org ) at 2015-01-13 19:42 CST
Nmap scan report for 192.168.1.1
Host is up (0.00090s latency).
Not shown: 994 closed ports
PORT       STATE SERVICE
53/tcp     open  domain
139/tcp    open  netbios-ssn
445/tcp    open  microsoft-ds
548/tcp    open  afp
5009/tcp   open  airport-admin
10000/tcp  open  snet-sensor-mgmt
[...]

Nmap done: 3 IP addresses (3 hosts up) scanned in 22.15 seconds
```

Nmap scan using a list for target specification

The resulting scan displayed above will be performed for each host in the list.txt file. This is useful for situations where you want to scan a large number of targets that would be cumbersome when attempting to string them together as command line arguments.

Scan Random Targets

The -iR parameter can be used to select random internet hosts to scan. Nmap will randomly generate the specified number of targets and attempt to scan them.

Usage syntax: nmap -iR [number of targets]

```
$ nmap -iR 3

Starting Nmap 6.47 ( http://nmap.org ) at 2015-01-13 19:44 CST

[...]

Nmap done: 3 IP addresses (1 host up) scanned in 14.53 seconds
```

Scanning three randomly generated IP addresses

Note: For privacy reasons the results of the above scan are not displayed in this book.

Executing nmap -iR 3 instructs Nmap to randomly generate 3 IP addresses to scan. There aren't many good reasons to ever do a random scan unless you are working on a research project (or just really bored). Additionally, if you do a lot of aggressive random scanning you could end up getting in trouble with your internet service provider as many have started to monitor customer connections for suspicious network activity. You could get a warning or even banned if network scanning is prohibited by your provider's terms of service. In most cases, however, light scanning will not raise any red flags.

Exclude Targets from a Scan

The --exclude option is used with Nmap to exclude hosts from a scan.

Usage syntax: nmap [targets] --exclude [target(s)]

```
$ nmap 192.168.1.0/24 --exclude 192.168.1.1

Starting Nmap 6.47 ( http://nmap.org ) at 2015-01-13 19:53 CST

[...]

Nmap done: 255 IP addresses (7 hosts up) scanned in 49.33 seconds
```

Excluding a single IP from a scan

The --exclude option is useful if you want to exclude specific hosts when scanning a large number of addresses. In the example above host 192.168.1.1 is excluded from the group of targets being scanned.

The --exclude option accepts single hosts, ranges, or entire network blocks (using CIDR notation) as demonstrated in the next example.

```
$ nmap 192.168.1.0/24 --exclude 192.168.1.1-100

Starting Nmap 6.47 ( http://nmap.org ) at 2015-01-13 19:57 CST

[...]

Nmap done: 156 IP addresses (5 hosts up) scanned in 48.79 seconds
```

Excluding a range of IP addresses from a scan

In the example above, 256 addresses are specified using CIDR and a range of 100 addresses are excluded, which results in 156 addresses being scanned.

Exclude Targets Using a List

The --excludefile option is related to the --exclude option and can be used to provide a list of targets to exclude from a network scan.

```
$ cat list.txt
192.168.1.1
192.168.1.5
192.168.1.100
```

Text file with hosts to exclude from a scan

The example below demonstrates using the --excludefile argument to exclude the hosts in the list.txt file displayed above.

Usage syntax: nmap [targets] --excludefile [list.txt]

```
$ nmap 192.168.1.0/24 --excludefile list.txt

Starting Nmap 6.47 ( http://nmap.org ) at 2015-01-13 20:01 CST
Nmap scan report for 192.168.1.101
Host is up (0.0098s latency).
Not shown: 995 closed ports
PORT       STATE SERVICE
3689/tcp   open  rendezvous
5000/tcp   open  upnp
7000/tcp   open  afs3-fileserver
7100/tcp   open  font-service
62078/tcp  open  iphone-sync
[...]

Nmap done: 253 IP addresses (5 hosts up) scanned in 81.09 seconds
```

Excluding a list of hosts from a network scan

In the above example, the targets in the list.txt file are excluded from the scan. You can utilize this feature to add systems on your network that you don't want to disturb while performing an audit.

57

Perform an Aggressive Scan

The -A parameter instructs Nmap to perform an aggressive scan.

Usage syntax: nmap -A [target]

```
# nmap -A 10.10.4.31

Starting Nmap 6.47 ( http://nmap.org ) at 2015-01-16 09:10 CST
Nmap scan report for 10.10.4.31
Host is up (0.0031s latency).
Not shown: 999 closed ports
PORT   STATE SERVICE VERSION
80/tcp open  http    3Com switch http config
| http-title: Web user login
|_Requested resource was index.htm
MAC Address: CC:3E:5F:5B:BE:80 (Hewlett Packard)
Device type: switch
Running: H3C Comware 5.X
OS CPE: cpe:/o:h3c:comware:5.20
OS details: H3C Comware 5.20
Network Distance: 1 hop
Service Info: Device: switch

TRACEROUTE
HOP RTT     ADDRESS
1   3.08 ms 10.10.4.31

OS and Service detection performed. Please report any incorrect
results at http://nmap.org/submit/ .
Nmap done: 1 IP address (1 host up) scanned in 27.95 seconds
```

Output of an aggressive scan

The aggressive scan selects some of the most commonly used options within Nmap and is provided as a simple alternative to typing a long string of command line arguments. The -A parameter is a synonym for several advanced options (like -O -sC --traceroute) which can also be accessed individually and are covered later in this guide. The resulting output includes more information than what is shown in a typical Nmap scan such as the device type and operating system.

Scan an IPv6 Target

The -6 parameter is used to perform a scan of an IP version 6 target.

Usage syntax: nmap -6 [target]

```
# nmap -6 fe80::2572:dd3a:34fe:daa9

Starting Nmap 6.47 ( http://nmap.org ) at 2015-01-14 15:10 CST

Nmap scan report for myserver (fe80::2572:dd3a:34fe:daa9)
Host is up (0.0011s latency).
Not shown: 988 closed ports
PORT       STATE SERVICE
80/tcp     open  http
135/tcp    open  msrpc
445/tcp    open  microsoft-ds
1099/tcp   open  rmiregistry
1521/tcp   open  oracle
3389/tcp   open  ms-wbt-server
5080/tcp   open  onscreen
8080/tcp   open  http-proxy
9999/tcp   open  abyss
49152/tcp  open  unknown
49153/tcp  open  unknown
49154/tcp  open  unknown
MAC Address: 00:0C:29:C2:E7:8E (VMware)

Nmap done: 1 IP address (1 host up) scanned in 6.45 seconds
```

Scanning an IPv6 address

The example above displays the results of scanning an IP version 6 system. Most Nmap options support IPv6 with the exception of multiple target scanning using ranges and CIDR, as they are pointless on IPv6 networks.

Note: *The host, target, and interconnecting systems must all support the IPv6 protocol in order for a -6 scan to work.*

Section 3: Discovery Options

Overview

Before port scanning a target, Nmap will attempt to send ICMP echo requests to see if the host is "alive." This can save time when scanning multiple hosts as Nmap will not waste time attempting to probe hosts that are not online. Because ICMP requests are often blocked by firewalls, Nmap will also check TCP ports 80 and 443 since these common web server ports are often open (even if ICMP is not).

The default discovery options aren't always useful when scanning secured systems. The following section describes alternative methods for host discovery that allow you to perform custom discovery pings when looking for available targets.

Summary of features covered in this section:

-Pn (formerly –PN)
Don't Ping

-sn (formerly -sP)
Perform a Ping Only Scan

-PS
TCP SYN Ping

-PA
TCP ACK Ping

-PU
UDP Ping

-PE
ICMP Echo Ping

-PP
ICMP Timestamp Ping

-PM
ICMP Address Mask Ping

-PO
IP Protocol Ping

-PR
ARP Ping

--traceroute
Traceroute

-n
Disable Reverse DNS Resolution

--system-dns
Alternative DNS Lookup

--dns-servers
Manually Specify DNS Server(s)

-sL
Create a Host List

Don't Ping

By default, before Nmap attempts to scan a system for open ports it will first ping the target to see if it is online. This feature helps save time when scanning as it causes targets that do not respond to be skipped.

```
$ nmap 10.10.5.139

Starting Nmap 6.47 ( http://nmap.org ) at 2015-01-15 10:06 CST
Note: Host seems down. If it is really up, but blocking our ping
probes, try -Pn
Nmap done: 1 IP address (0 hosts up) scanned in 3.07 seconds
```

Results of an Nmap scan where the target system is not pingable

In the above example the specified target is not scanned because it does not respond to Nmap's pings. The -Pn option instructs Nmap to skip the default discovery check and perform a complete port scan on the target. This is useful when scanning systems that are protected by a firewall that blocks ping probes.

Usage syntax: nmap -Pn [target]

```
$ nmap -Pn 10.10.5.139

Starting Nmap 6.47 ( http://nmap.org ) at 2015-01-15 10:07 CST
Nmap scan report for 10.10.5.139
Host is up (0.0020s latency).
Not shown: 997 filtered ports
PORT      STATE SERVICE
135/tcp   open  msrpc
5800/tcp  open  vnc-http
5900/tcp  open  vnc

Nmap done: 1 IP address (1 host up) scanned in 4.90 seconds
```

Output of a Nmap scan with ping discovery disabled

By specifying the -Pn option on the same target, Nmap is able to produce a list of open ports on the un-pingable system.

Note: *The -Pn option was -PN in Nmap version 5 and earlier. It was renamed for consistency.*

Ping Only Scan

The -sn option is used to perform a simple ping of the specified target (without scanning any ports).

Usage syntax: nmap -sn [target]

```
$ nmap -sn 192.168.1.0/24

Starting Nmap 6.47 ( http://nmap.org ) at 2015-01-13 20:12 CST
Nmap scan report for 192.168.1.1
Host is up (0.0017s latency).
Nmap scan report for 192.168.1.5
Host is up (0.0011s latency).
Nmap scan report for 192.168.1.100
Host is up (0.0020s latency).
Nmap scan report for 192.168.1.101
Host is up (0.010s latency).
Nmap scan report for 192.168.1.105
Host is up (0.0011s latency).
Nmap scan report for 192.168.1.109
Host is up (0.0011s latency).
Nmap scan report for 192.168.1.111
Host is up (0.000066s latency).
Nmap done: 256 IP addresses (7 hosts up) scanned in 2.32 seconds
```

Output of a ping only scan

The -sn option is useful when you want to perform a quick search of the target network to see which hosts are online without actually scanning the systems for open ports. In the above example, all valid addresses in the 192.168.1.0/24 subnet are pinged and results from responding hosts are displayed.

When scanning a local network, you can execute Nmap with root privileges for additional ping functionality. When doing this, the -sn option will perform an ARP ping and return the MAC addresses of the discovered system(s).

Note: *This is the default behavior on Windows systems.*

```
$ sudo nmap -sn 192.168.1.0/24
[sudo] password for nick: ******

Starting Nmap 6.47 ( http://nmap.org ) at 2015-01-13 20:14 CST
Nmap scan report for 192.168.1.1
Host is up (0.00075s latency).
MAC Address: 6C:70:9F:D6:2D:94 (Apple)
[...]
Nmap done: 256 IP addresses (7 hosts up) scanned in 1.80 seconds
```

Output of a ping only scan (as root)

Note: *The -sn option was -sP in Nmap version 5 and earlier. It was renamed for consistency.*

TCP SYN Ping

The -PS option performs a TCP SYN ping.

Usage syntax: nmap -PS[port1,port1,etc] [target]

```
# nmap -PS 10.10.3.1

Starting Nmap 6.47 ( http://nmap.org ) at 2015-01-14 15:14 CST
Nmap scan report for 10.10.3.1
Host is up (0.045s latency).
Not shown: 997 closed ports
PORT     STATE SERVICE
22/tcp   open  ssh
80/tcp   open  http
443/tcp  open  https

Nmap done: 1 IP address (1 host up) scanned in 0.61 seconds
```

Performing a TCP SYN ping

The -PS options sends an SYN packet to the target system and listens for a response. A SYN packet is the first part of what's known as a TCP three-way handshake. Any system with an open or unfiltered TCP port will respond to this type of probe. This alternative discovery method is useful for systems that are configured to block standard ICMP pings.

Note: *The default port for -PS is 80, but others can be specified using the following syntax: nmap -PS22,25,80,443,etc. This can be useful for trying to solicit a response from a system that is filtering port 80.*

TCP ACK Ping

The -PA performs a TCP ACK ping on the specified target.

Usage syntax: nmap -PA[port1,port1,etc] [target]

```
$ nmap -PA 10.10.3.1

Starting Nmap 6.47 ( http://nmap.org ) at 2015-01-14 15:15 CST
Nmap scan report for 10.10.3.1
Host is up (0.055s latency).
Not shown: 997 closed ports
PORT     STATE SERVICE
22/tcp   open  ssh
80/tcp   open  http
443/tcp  open  https

Nmap done: 1 IP address (1 host up) scanned in 0.57 seconds
```

Performing a TCP ACK ping

The -PA option causes Nmap to send TCP ACK packets to the specified hosts. This method attempts to discover hosts by appearing to respond to TCP connections that don't actually exist in an attempt to solicit a response from the target. Like other ping options, it is useful in situations where standard ICMP pings are blocked.

Note: *The default port for -PA is 80, but others can be specified using the following syntax: nmap -PA22,25,80,443,etc.*

UDP Ping

The -PU option performs a UDP ping on the target system.

Usage syntax: nmap -PU[port1,port1,etc] [target]

```
# nmap -PU 10.10.4.59

Starting Nmap 6.47 ( http://nmap.org ) at 2015-01-14 15:18 CST
Nmap scan report for 10.10.4.59
Host is up (0.0023s latency).
Not shown: 992 closed ports
PORT       STATE SERVICE
21/tcp     open  ftp
22/tcp     open  ssh
23/tcp     open  telnet
80/tcp     open  http
161/tcp    open  snmp
515/tcp    open  printer
9100/tcp   open  jetdirect
9200/tcp   open  wap-wsp

Nmap done: 1 IP address (1 host up) scanned in 13.98 seconds
```

Performing a UDP ping

This discovery method sends UDP packets in an attempt to solicit a response from a target. While most firewalled systems will block this type of connection, some poorly configured systems may allow it if they are only configured to filter TCP connections.

Note: *The default port for -PU is 40125. Others can be specified by using the following syntax: nmap -PU22,25,80,443,etc.*

ICMP Echo Ping

The -PE option performs an ICMP (Internet Control Message Protocol) echo ping on the specified system.

Usage syntax: nmap -PE [target]

```
# nmap -PE 10.10.4.59

Starting Nmap 6.47 ( http://nmap.org ) at 2015-01-14 15:23 CST
Nmap scan report for 10.10.4.59
Host is up (0.0028s latency).
Not shown: 992 closed ports
PORT      STATE SERVICE
21/tcp    open  ftp
22/tcp    open  ssh
23/tcp    open  telnet
80/tcp    open  http
161/tcp   open  snmp
515/tcp   open  printer
9100/tcp  open  jetdirect
9200/tcp  open  wap-wsp

Nmap done: 1 IP address (1 host up) scanned in 3.53 seconds
```

Performing an ICMP echo ping

The -PE option sends a standard ICMP ping to the target to see if it replies. This type of discovery works best on local networks where ICMP packets can be transmitted with few restrictions. Many internet hosts, however, are configured not to respond to ICMP packets for security reasons.

Note: *The -PE option is automatically implied if no other ping options are specified.*

ICMP Timestamp Ping

The -PP option performs an ICMP timestamp ping.

Usage syntax: nmap -PP [target]

```
# nmap -PP 10.10.4.59

Starting Nmap 6.47 ( http://nmap.org ) at 2015-01-14 15:24 CST
Nmap scan report for 10.10.4.59
Host is up (0.0029s latency).
Not shown: 992 closed ports
PORT      STATE SERVICE
21/tcp    open  ftp
22/tcp    open  ssh
23/tcp    open  telnet
80/tcp    open  http
161/tcp   open  snmp
515/tcp   open  printer
9100/tcp  open  jetdirect
9200/tcp  open  wap-wsp

Nmap done: 1 IP address (1 host up) scanned in 3.50 seconds
```

Performing an ICMP timestamp ping

While most firewalled systems are configured to block ICMP echo requests, some improperly configured systems may still reply to ICMP timestamp requests. This makes the -PP option useful when attempting to solicit responses from firewalled targets.

ICMP Address Mask Ping

The -PM option performs an ICMP address mask ping.

Usage syntax: nmap -PM [target]

```
# nmap -PM 10.10.4.59

Starting Nmap 6.47 ( http://nmap.org ) at 2015-01-14 15:25 CST
Nmap scan report for 10.10.4.59
Host is up (0.0036s latency).
Not shown: 992 closed ports
PORT      STATE SERVICE
21/tcp    open  ftp
22/tcp    open  ssh
23/tcp    open  telnet
80/tcp    open  http
161/tcp   open  snmp
515/tcp   open  printer
9100/tcp  open  jetdirect
9200/tcp  open  wap-wsp

Nmap done: 1 IP address (1 host up) scanned in 3.52 seconds
```

Performing an ICMP address mask ping

This unconventional ICMP query (similar to the -PP option) attempts to ping the specified host using alternative ICMP registers. This type of ping can occasionally sneak past a firewall that is configured to only block standard echo requests.

IP Protocol Ping

The -PO option performs an IP protocol ping.

Usage syntax: nmap -PO[protocol1,protocol2,etc] [target]

```
# nmap -PO1 10.10.3.1

Starting Nmap 6.47 ( http://nmap.org ) at 2015-01-16 10:28 CST
Nmap scan report for 10.10.3.1
Host is up (0.14s latency).
Not shown: 997 closed ports
PORT     STATE SERVICE
22/tcp   open  ssh
80/tcp   open  http
443/tcp  open  https

Nmap done: 1 IP address (1 host up) scanned in 17.74 seconds
```

Performing an IP protocol ping

An IP protocol ping sends packets with the specified protocol to the target. If no protocols are specified, the default protocols 1 (ICMP), 2 (IGMP), and 4 (IP) are used. To ping using a custom set of protocols, use nmap -PO1,2,4,etc. This type of ping can sometimes get a target to respond with ICMP unreachable messages if the type of protocol used is not supported.

Note: *A complete list of Internet Protocol numbers can be found online at iana.org/assignments/protocol-numbers.*

ARP Ping

The -PR option instructs Nmap to perform an ARP (Address Resolution Protocol) ping on the specified target.

Usage syntax: nmap -PR [target]

```
# nmap -PR 10.10.4.59

Starting Nmap 6.47 ( http://nmap.org ) at 2015-01-14 15:31 CST
Nmap scan report for 10.10.4.59
Host is up (0.0077s latency).
Not shown: 992 closed ports
PORT      STATE SERVICE
21/tcp    open  ftp
22/tcp    open  ssh
23/tcp    open  telnet
80/tcp    open  http
161/tcp   open  snmp
515/tcp   open  printer
9100/tcp  open  jetdirect
9200/tcp  open  wap-wsp
MAC Address: 00:10:40:57:80:17 (Intermec)

Nmap done: 1 IP address (1 host up) scanned in 1.63 seconds
```

Performing an ARP ping

The -PR option is automatically implied when scanning the local network with root access. This type of discovery is much faster than the other ping methods described in this guide. It also has the added benefit of being more accurate because LAN hosts can't block ARP requests (even if they are running a firewall) since it is an essential feature of ethernet networks. As shown above, the ARP ping will also display the MAC address of the target system.

Note: *ARP scans cannot be performed on targets that are not on your local subnet. On Linux systems you must use root privileges for ARP scans to work properly. The -PR option is technically redundant because it is the default type of ping on LANs. Interestingly, Nmap will silently override all other discovery options when scanning the local network. If you <u>really</u> want to experiment with the other discovery options on a LAN you must use the --disable-arp-ping option.*

Traceroute

The --traceroute parameter can be used to trace the network path to the specified host.

Usage syntax: nmap --traceroute [target]

```
# nmap --traceroute scanme.nmap.org

Starting Nmap 6.47 ( http://nmap.org ) at 2015-01-15 20:47 CST

[...]

TRACEROUTE (using port 587/tcp)
HOP RTT      ADDRESS
1   5.00 ms  192.168.1.1
2   14.00 ms 10.33.112.1
3   14.00 ms 70.183.70.198
4   25.00 ms 70.183.71.104
5   24.00 ms 70.183.71.104
6   43.00 ms wichsysr02.rd.ks.cox.net (70.183.71.8)
7   54.00 ms 68.1.2.109
8   39.00 ms v209.core1.dal1.he.net (184.105.16.77)
9   91.00 ms 10ge9-1.core3.fmt2.he.net (72.52.92.153)
10  85.00 ms router4-fmt.linode.com (64.71.132.138)
11  82.00 ms scanme.nmap.org (74.207.244.221)

Nmap done: 1 IP address (1 host up) scanned in 6.07 seconds
```

Output of a traceroute scan

The --traceroute option performs a trace of routes used to reach the specified target. Each router or "HOP" along the way is displayed along with the round trip time (RTT). Nmap will also attempt to perform a reverse DNS lookup and display any responses, which can reveal interesting information about the routers between you and the destination.

The information displayed is similar to the traceroute or tracepath commands found on Unix and Linux systems (Windows uses tracert). Nmap has the added bonus of its tracing being functionally superior to these commands because it is generally much faster and more accurate than other route tracing programs.

Disable Reverse DNS Resolution

The -n parameter is used to disable reverse DNS lookups.

Usage syntax: nmap -n [target]

```
$ nmap -n 74.207.244.221

Starting Nmap 6.47 ( http://nmap.org ) at 2015-01-15 09:36 CST
Nmap scan report for 74.207.244.221
Host is up (0.059s latency).
Not shown: 997 closed ports
PORT      STATE SERVICE
22/tcp    open  ssh
80/tcp    open  http
9929/tcp  open  nping-echo

Nmap done: 1 IP address (1 host up) scanned in 1.04 seconds
```

Output of an Nmap scan with reverse DNS disabled

Reverse DNS can significantly slow the performance of an Nmap scan. Using the -n option can greatly reduce scanning times – especially when scanning a large number of hosts. This option is useful if you don't care about the DNS information for the target system and prefer to perform a scan that produces faster results. In the example above, the -n option prevents Nmap from attempting to resolve the specified IP address.

Alternative DNS Lookup Method

The --system-dns option instructs Nmap to use the host system's DNS resolver instead of its own internal method.

Usage syntax: nmap --system-dns [target]

```
# nmap --system-dns scanme.nmap.org

Starting Nmap 6.47 ( http://nmap.org ) at 2015-01-21 15:07 CST
Nmap scan report for scanme.nmap.org (74.207.244.221)
Host is up (0.12s latency).
Not shown: 997 closed ports
PORT      STATE SERVICE
22/tcp    open  ssh
80/tcp    open  http
9929/tcp  open  nping-echo

Nmap done: 1 IP address (1 host up) scanned in 5.79 seconds
```

Output of an Nmap scan using the system DNS resolver

This option is rarely used because it is much slower than the default method. It can, however, be useful when troubleshooting DNS problems with Nmap.

Note: *The system resolver is always used for IPv6 scans.*

Manually Specify DNS Server(s)

The --dns-servers option is used to manually specify DNS servers to be queried when scanning.

Usage syntax: nmap --dns-servers [server1,server2,etc] [target]

```
# nmap --dns-servers 8.8.8.8,8.8.4.4 scanme.nmap.org

Starting Nmap 6.47 ( http://nmap.org ) at 2015-01-21 15:08 CST
Nmap scan report for scanme.nmap.org (74.207.244.221)
Host is up (0.43s latency).
Not shown: 997 closed ports
PORT     STATE SERVICE
22/tcp   open  ssh
80/tcp   open  http
9929/tcp open  nping-echo

Nmap done: 1 IP address (1 host up) scanned in 4.98 seconds
```

Manually specifying DNS servers

Nmap's default behavior will use the DNS servers configured on your local system for name resolution. The --dns-servers option allows you to specify one or more alternative servers for Nmap to query. This can be useful for systems that do not have DNS configured or if you want to prevent your scan lookups from appearing in your locally configured DNS server's log file.

Create a Host List

The -sL option performs a reverse DNS lookup of the specified IP addresses.

Usage syntax: nmap -sL [target]

```
$ nmap -sL 8.8.4.4 8.8.8.8 74.207.244.221

Starting Nmap 6.47 ( http://nmap.org ) at 2015-01-16 10:47 CST
Nmap scan report for google-public-dns-b.google.com (8.8.4.4)
Nmap scan report for google-public-dns-a.google.com (8.8.8.8)
Nmap scan report for scanme.nmap.org (74.207.244.221)
Nmap done: 3 IP addresses (0 hosts up) scanned in 0.00 seconds
```

Output of a host list generated by Nmap

The -sL scan does not send any packets to the target systems. Instead, it performs a reverse DNS lookup of the specified IP addresses. The above scan shows the results of the reverse lookup for the specified systems. Many DNS names can reveal interesting information about an IP address, including what it's used for or where it is located.

Section 4: Advanced Scanning Options

Overview

Nmap supports a number of user selectable scan types. By default, Nmap will perform a basic TCP scan on each target system. In some situations, it may be necessary to perform a more complex TCP (or even UDP) scan in an attempt to find uncommon services or evade a firewall. Nmap's options for these advanced scan types are discussed in this section.

Summary of features covered in this section:

-sS
TCP SYN Scan

-sT
TCP Connect Scan

-sU
UDP Scan

-sN
TCP NULL Scan

-sF
TCP FIN Scan

-sX
Xmas Scan

-sA
TCP ACK Scan

--scanflags
Custom TCP Scan

-sO
IP Protocol Scan

Note: *You must login with root privileges (or use the sudo command) to execute many of the scans discussed in this section.*

TCP SYN Scan

The -sS option performs a TCP SYN scan.

Usage syntax: nmap -sS [target]

```
# nmap -sS 10.10.3.1

Starting Nmap 6.47 ( http://nmap.org ) at 2015-01-15 09:45 CST
Nmap scan report for 10.10.3.1
Host is up (0.14s latency).
Not shown: 997 closed ports
PORT     STATE SERVICE
22/tcp   open  ssh
80/tcp   open  http
443/tcp  open  https

Nmap done: 1 IP address (1 host up) scanned in 0.58 seconds
```

Performing a TCP SYN scan

The TCP SYN scan is the default option for privileged users (users running as root on Unix/Linux). The default TCP SYN scan attempts to identify the 1000 most commonly used TCP ports by sending a SYN packet to the target and listening for a response. This type of scan is said to be stealthy because it does not attempt to open a full-fledged connection to the remote host. This prevents some systems from logging a connection attempt of your scan.

Note: *Stealth operation is not guaranteed. Modern packet capture programs and advanced firewalls are now able to detect TCP SYN scans.*

TCP Connect Scan

The -sT option performs a TCP connect scan.

Usage syntax: nmap -sT [target]

```
$ nmap -sT 10.10.3.1

Starting Nmap 6.47 ( http://nmap.org ) at 2015-01-15 09:52 CST
Nmap scan report for 10.10.3.1
Host is up (0.048s latency).
Not shown: 997 closed ports
PORT     STATE SERVICE
22/tcp   open  ssh
80/tcp   open  http
443/tcp  open  https

Nmap done: 1 IP address (1 host up) scanned in 1.98 seconds
```

Performing a TCP connect scan

The -sT scan is the default scan type for non-privileged users. The TCP connect scan is a simple probe that attempts to directly connect to the remote system without using any stealth options. The -sT option utilizes the local system's TCP/IP stack rather than generating its own raw packets. This can be slower and less accurate. Thus, it is typically best to execute Nmap with root privileges whenever possible as it will perform a TCP SYN scan (-sS) which can provide a more accurate listing of port states (and is significantly faster).

UDP Scan

The -sU option performs a UDP (User Datagram Protocol) scan.

Usage syntax: nmap -sU [target]

```
# nmap -sU 10.10.3.1

Starting Nmap 6.47 ( http://nmap.org ) at 2015-01-15 09:53 CST
Nmap scan report for 10.10.3.1
Host is up (0.0023s latency).
Not shown: 998 open|filtered ports
PORT     STATE  SERVICE
161/udp  open   snmp
162/udp  closed snmptrap

Nmap done: 1 IP address (1 host up) scanned in 1.20 seconds
```

Performing a UDP scan

The example above displays the results of a UDP scan. While TCP is the most commonly used transport protocol, many network services like DNS, DHCP, and SNMP still utilize UDP. When performing a network audit, it's always a good idea to check for both TCP and UDP services to get a more complete picture of the target systems. The next example shows the output of a combination TCP/UDP scan.

```
# nmap -sS -sU 10.10.3.1

Starting Nmap 6.47 ( http://nmap.org ) at 2015-01-16 11:27 CST
Nmap scan report for 10.10.3.1
Host is up (0.044s latency).
Not shown: 998 closed ports, 998 open|filtered ports
PORT     STATE SERVICE
22/tcp   open  ssh
80/tcp   open  http
443/tcp  open  https
161/udp  open  snmp

Nmap done: 1 IP address (1 host up) scanned in 6.04 seconds
```

Performing a TCP and UDP scan

By combining options for both TCP and UDP, you are able to see open ports that might otherwise go unnoticed if only scanning for one protocol.

Note: *UDP scans are typically slower than TCP scans because UDP ports behave differently than TCP (by design). Additionally, many systems also utilize rate limiting for UDP responses, which greatly reduces UDP scan performance.*

TCP NULL Scan

The -sN option performs a TCP NULL scan.

Usage syntax: nmap -sN [target]

```
# nmap -sN 10.10.4.85

Starting Nmap 6.47 ( http://nmap.org ) at 2015-01-15 10:05 CST
Nmap scan report for 10.10.4.85
Host is up (0.00052s latency).
Not shown: 996 closed ports
PORT        STATE           SERVICE
22/tcp      open|filtered   ssh
80/tcp      open|filtered   http
443/tcp     open|filtered   https
17988/tcp   open|filtered   unknown
MAC Address: D8:9D:67:60:32:57 (Hewlett Packard)

Nmap done: 1 IP address (1 host up) scanned in 7.52 seconds
```

Performing a TCP NULL scan

A TCP NULL scan causes Nmap to send packets with no TCP flags enabled. This is achieved by setting the header to 0. Sending NULL packets to a target is a method of tricking a firewalled system to generate a response, although Nmap may not be able to determine the port state (as shown in the above example). Additionally, not all systems will respond to probes of this type.

TCP FIN Scan

The -sF option performs a TCP FIN scan.

Usage syntax: nmap -sF [target]

```
# nmap -sF 10.10.4.85

Starting Nmap 6.47 ( http://nmap.org ) at 2015-01-15 10:43 CST
Nmap scan report for 10.10.4.85
Host is up (0.00052s latency).
Not shown: 996 closed ports
PORT       STATE            SERVICE
22/tcp     open|filtered    ssh
80/tcp     open|filtered    http
443/tcp    open|filtered    https
17988/tcp  open|filtered    unknown
MAC Address: D8:9D:67:60:32:57 (Hewlett Packard)

Nmap done: 1 IP address (1 host up) scanned in 6.78 seconds
```

Performing a TCP FIN scan

In a -sF scan, Nmap marks the TCP FIN bit active when sending packets in an attempt to solicit a response from the specified target system. This is another method of sending unexpected packets to a target in an attempt to produce results from a system protected by a firewall.

Note: *Not all systems will respond to probes of this type.*

Xmas Scan

The -sX flag performs a Xmas scan.

Usage syntax: nmap -sX [target]

```
# nmap -sX 10.10.4.85

Starting Nmap 6.47 ( http://nmap.org ) at 2015-01-15 10:46 CST
Nmap scan report for 10.10.4.85
Host is up (0.00053s latency).
Not shown: 996 closed ports
PORT       STATE         SERVICE
22/tcp     open|filtered ssh
80/tcp     open|filtered http
443/tcp    open|filtered https
17988/tcp  open|filtered unknown
MAC Address: D8:9D:67:60:32:57 (Hewlett Packard)

Nmap done: 1 IP address (1 host up) scanned in 2.57 seconds
```

Performing a "Christmas" scan

In the Xmas scan, Nmap sends TCP packets with URG, FIN, and PSH flags activated. This has the effect of "lighting the packet up like a Christmas tree" and can occasionally solicit a response from a firewalled system that might otherwise ignore a normal packet.

Note: *Not all systems will respond to probes of this type.*

Custom TCP Scan

The --scanflags option is used to perform a custom TCP scan by setting your own header flags.

Usage syntax: nmap --scanflags [flag(s)] [target]

```
# nmap --scanflags SYNURG 10.10.3.1

Starting Nmap 6.47 ( http://nmap.org ) at 2015-01-15 10:49 CST
Nmap scan report for 10.10.3.1
Host is up (0.046s latency).
Not shown: 997 closed ports
PORT     STATE SERVICE
22/tcp   open  ssh
80/tcp   open  http
443/tcp  open  https

Nmap done: 1 IP address (1 host up) scanned in 0.57 seconds
```

Manually specifying TCP flags

The --scanflags option allows users to define a custom scan using one or more TCP header flags. This allows you to shape your own TCP headers in an attempt to get a response from a target system. Any combination of flags listed in the table below can be used with the --scanflags option. For example: nmap --scanflags FINACK (no space) would activate the FIN and ACK TCP flags.

TCP header flags:

SYN - Synchronize

ACK - Acknowledgment

PSH - Push

URG - Urgent

RST - Reset

FIN - Finished

TCP ACK Scan

The -sA option performs a TCP ACK scan.

Usage syntax: nmap -sA [target]

```
# nmap -sA 10.10.4.1 10.10.4.106

Starting Nmap 6.47 ( http://nmap.org ) at 2015-01-16 13:30 CST

Nmap scan report for 10.10.4.1
Host is up (0.0014s latency).
All 1000 scanned ports on 10.10.4.1 are unfiltered
MAC Address: 00:13:3B:10:54:0E (Speed Dragon Multimedia Limited)

Nmap scan report for 10.10.4.106
Host is up (0.0020s latency).
All 1000 scanned ports on 10.10.4.106 are filtered
MAC Address: 2C:27:D7:42:E7:25 (Hewlett-Packard Company)

Nmap done: 2 IP addresses (2 hosts up) scanned in 4.91 seconds
```

Performing a TCP ACK scan

The -sA option can be used to determine if the target system is protected by a firewall. When performing a TCP ACK scan, Nmap will probe a target and look for RST responses. If no response is received, the system is considered to be filtered. If the system does return an RST packet, then it is labeled as unfiltered. In the above example, two systems are scanned. One appears to be filtered and the other does not.

Note: *The -sA option does not display whether or not the unfiltered ports are open or closed. Its only purpose is to determine whether or not the system is performing filtering.*

IP Protocol Scan

The -sO option performs an IP protocol scan.

Usage syntax: nmap -sO [target]

```
# nmap -sO 10.10.4.49

Starting Nmap 6.47 ( http://nmap.org ) at 2015-01-16 13:34 CST
Nmap scan report for 10.10.4.49
Host is up (0.012s latency).
Not shown: 253 open|filtered protocols
PROTOCOL  STATE  SERVICE
1         open   icmp
6         open   tcp
17        open   udp
MAC Address: EC:E1:A9:54:1B:80 (Cisco)

Nmap done: 1 IP address (1 host up) scanned in 7.30 seconds
```

Output of an IP protocol scan

The -sO scan displays the IP protocols that are supported on the target system. The most commonly found protocols on modern networks are ICMP, TCP, and UDP, as displayed in the above example. The IP protocol scan is helpful for quickly identifying what types of scans you want to perform on the selected target system based on its supported protocols.

Tip: *A complete list of IP protocols can be found on the IANA website at iana.org/assignments/protocol-numbers/.*

Section 5: Port Scanning Options

Overview

There are a total of 65,535 ports used in TCP/IP. Nmap, by default, only scans 1,000 of the most commonly used ports. This is done to save time when scanning multiple targets, as the majority of ports outside the top 1,000 are rarely used. Sometimes, however, you may want to scan outside the default range of ports to look for uncommon services or ports that have been forwarded to a different location. This section covers the options that allow this and other port specific features.

Tip: A complete list of TCP/IP ports can be found on the IANA website at *iana.org/assignments/port-numbers*.

Summary of features covered in this section:

-F
Perform a Fast Scan

-p [port]
Scan Specific Ports

-p [name]
Scan Ports by Name

-p U:[UDP ports],T:[TCP ports]
Scan Ports by Protocol

-p "*"
Scan All Ports

--top-ports [number]
Scan Top Ports

-r
Perform a Sequential Port Scan

--open
Only display open ports

Perform a Fast Scan

The -F option instructs Nmap to perform a scan of only the 100 most commonly used ports.

Usage syntax: nmap -F [target]

```
$ nmap -F 10.10.4.48

Starting Nmap 6.47 ( http://nmap.org ) at 2015-01-15 11:05 CST
Nmap scan report for 10.10.4.48
Host is up (0.0018s latency).
Not shown: 96 closed ports
PORT      STATE SERVICE
80/tcp    open  http
111/tcp   open  rpcbind
2049/tcp  open  nfs
5000/tcp  open  upnp

Nmap done: 1 IP address (1 host up) scanned in 0.10 seconds
```

Output of a "fast" scan

Nmap scans the top 1,000 commonly used TCP ports by default. The -F option reduces that number to 100. The top 100 ports include some of the most common network services like DNS, SMTP, and HTTP. This can dramatically speed up scanning while still representing the majority of commonly used ports.

Scan Specific Ports

The -p option is used to instruct Nmap to scan the specified port(s).

Usage syntax: nmap [port1,port2,etc|range of ports] [target]

```
$ nmap -p 80 10.10.4.26

Starting Nmap 6.47 ( http://nmap.org ) at 2015-01-15 12:55 CST
Nmap scan report for 10.10.4.26
Host is up (0.000071s latency).
PORT   STATE SERVICE
80/tcp open  http

Nmap done: 1 IP address (1 host up) scanned in 0.06 seconds
```

Specifying a single port to scan

The example above demonstrates using -p to scan port 80 on a target system. This is useful when you are hunting for a specific service and don't want to bother with scanning all of the default ports. In addition to scanning a single port, you can scan multiple individual ports (separated by a comma) or a range of ports as demonstrated in the next example.

```
$ nmap -p 20-25,80,443 10.10.4.26

Starting Nmap 6.47 ( http://nmap.org ) at 2015-01-15 12:55 CST
Nmap scan report for 10.10.4.26
Host is up (0.00090s latency).
PORT    STATE  SERVICE
20/tcp  closed ftp-data
21/tcp  open   ftp
22/tcp  open   ssh
23/tcp  closed telnet
24/tcp  closed priv-mail
25/tcp  open   smtp
80/tcp  open   http
443/tcp open   https

Nmap done: 1 IP address (1 host up) scanned in 0.09 seconds
```

Specifying multiple ports to scan

In this example the -p option is used to scan ports 20 through 25, 80, and 443.

Scan Ports by Name

The -p option can also be used to scan ports by name.

Usage syntax: nmap -p [port name(s)] [target]

```
$ nmap -p smtp,http 10.10.4.26

Starting Nmap 6.47 ( http://nmap.org ) at 2015-01-15 12:57 CST
Nmap scan report for 10.10.4.26
Host is up (0.000069s latency).
PORT      STATE  SERVICE
25/tcp    open   smtp
80/tcp    open   http
8008/tcp  closed http

Nmap done: 1 IP address (1 host up) scanned in 0.04 seconds
```

Scanning ports by name

The example above demonstrates searching for open SMTP and HTTP ports by name using the -p option. The name(s) specified must match a service in the nmap-services file. This is usually found in /usr/local/share/nmap/ on Unix/Linux systems or C:\Program Files\Nmap\ on Windows systems.

Wildcards can also be used when specifying services by name. For example, using -p "http*" would scan for all ports that start with http (including http, https, and several others) as demonstrated below.

```
$ nmap -p "http*" 10.10.4.26

Starting Nmap 6.47 ( http://nmap.org ) at 2015-01-15 12:58 CST
Nmap scan report for 10.10.4.26
Host is up (0.00015s latency).
PORT      STATE  SERVICE
80/tcp    open   http
280/tcp   closed http-mgmt
443/tcp   open   https
591/tcp   closed http-alt
593/tcp   closed http-rpc-epmap
8000/tcp  closed http-alt
8008/tcp  closed http
8080/tcp  closed http-proxy
8443/tcp  closed https-alt

Nmap done: 1 IP address (1 host up) scanned in 0.09 seconds
```

Scanning ports by name using wildcards

Note: *Some systems may require you to enclose the wildcard statement in quotes so it is not interpreted as a shell wildcard.*

Scan Ports by Protocol

Specifying a T: or U: prefix with the -p option allows you to search for a specific port and protocol combination.

Usage syntax: nmap -p U:[UDP ports],T:[TCP ports] [target]

```
# nmap -sU -sT -p U:161,T:80 10.10.3.1

Starting Nmap 6.47 ( http://nmap.org ) at 2015-01-16 15:50 CST
Nmap scan report for 10.10.3.1
Host is up (0.0012s latency).
PORT     STATE SERVICE
80/tcp   open  http
161/udp  open  snmp

Nmap done: 1 IP address (1 host up) scanned in 1.30 seconds
```

Scanning specific ports by protocol

Using the syntax -p U:161,T:80 instructs Nmap to perform a UDP scan on port 161 and a TCP scan on port 80. This can reduce the amount of time spent scanning ports in situations where you know which ports are likely to respond to TCP and which will use UDP. In this case, the number of port/protocol combinations are cut in half when compared to simply running a scan with -p 80,161.

Note: *By default, Nmap will only scan TCP ports. In order to scan both TCP and UDP ports you will need to specify specific scan types such as -sU and -sT as shown in the example above.*

Scan All Ports

The -p- option is a catch-all used to scan all 65,535 ports on the specified target.

Usage syntax: nmap -p- [target]

```
# nmap -p- 10.10.4.80

Starting Nmap 6.47 ( http://nmap.org ) at 2015-02-08 15:36 CST
Nmap scan report for 10.10.4.80
Host is up (0.00029s latency).
Not shown: 65495 closed ports
PORT       STATE    SERVICE
[...]
8190/tcp   open     unknown
8191/tcp   open     unknown
8443/tcp   open     https-alt
9009/tcp   filtered pichat
9090/tcp   filtered zeus-admin
9443/tcp   open     tungsten-https
9875/tcp   filtered sapv1
10080/tcp  filtered unknown
10109/tcp  filtered unknown
10443/tcp  open     unknown
11711/tcp  open     unknown
11712/tcp  open     unknown
12443/tcp  open     unknown
12721/tcp  open     unknown
21000/tcp  filtered unknown
21100/tcp  open     unknown
22000/tcp  open     unknown
22100/tcp  open     unknown
48941/tcp  open     unknown
55969/tcp  open     unknown
59086/tcp  open     unknown
MAC Address: 00:50:56:BA:F8:B2 (VMware)

Nmap done: 1 IP address (1 host up) scanned in 18.48 seconds
```

Scanning all ports on a target system

Nmap only scans the top 1,000 ports by default. Scanning outside this range can open up the possibility of discovering services running on obscure ports. The above example shows some interesting ports listening outside of the well-known port numbers.

Tip: *Don't forget about UDP when scanning all ports. Including the -sU -sT options with -p- would scan all 65,535 ports using both TCP and UDP. This will take a considerable amount of time but will give you the most comprehensive port listing available for the target system.*

Scan Top Ports

The --top-ports option is used to scan the specified number of top ranked ports.

Usage syntax: nmap --top-ports [number] [target]

```
# nmap --top-ports 10 10.10.4.80

Starting Nmap 6.47 ( http://nmap.org ) at 2015-01-15 13:07 CST
Nmap scan report for 10.10.4.80
Host is up (0.00035s latency).
PORT     STATE  SERVICE
21/tcp   closed ftp
22/tcp   open   ssh
23/tcp   closed telnet
25/tcp   closed smtp
80/tcp   open   http
110/tcp  closed pop3
139/tcp  closed netbios-ssn
443/tcp  open   https
445/tcp  closed microsoft-ds
3389/tcp closed ms-wbt-server

Nmap done: 1 IP address (1 host up) scanned in 0.09 seconds
```

Performing a top port scan on the ten highest ranked ports

By default, Nmap will scan the 1000 most commonly used ports. The previously discussed -F option reduces that number to 100. Using the --top-ports option, you can specify any number of top ranked ports to scan.

The example above demonstrates using the --top-ports option to scan the top 10 ports. Any other number can be used to achieve the desired result. For example: nmap --top-ports 50 would scan the top 50 most commonly used ports and nmap --top-ports 500 would scan the top 500 most commonly used ports.

Perform a Sequential Port Scan

The -r option performs a sequential port scan on the specified target.

Usage syntax: nmap -r [target]

```
$ nmap -r 10.10.3.1

Starting Nmap 6.47 ( http://nmap.org ) at 2015-01-15 13:09 CST
Nmap scan report for 10.10.3.1
Host is up (0.043s latency).
Not shown: 997 closed ports
PORT     STATE SERVICE
22/tcp   open  ssh
80/tcp   open  http
443/tcp  open  https

Nmap done: 1 IP address (1 host up) scanned in 0.61 seconds
```

Performing a sequentially ordered port scan

Nmap's default scanning algorithm randomizes the port scan order. This is useful for evading firewalls and intrusion prevention systems. The -r parameter overrides this functionality and instructs Nmap to sequentially scan each port in numerical order.

Note: *The results of the -r scan aren't entirely evident because Nmap always sorts the final output of each scan. Combining the -v option with -r will display the sequential port discovery in real time.*

Only Display Open Ports

The --open parameter instructs Nmap to only display open ports.

Usage syntax: nmap --open [target]

```
$ nmap --open scanme.nmap.org

Starting Nmap 6.47 ( http://nmap.org ) at 2015-01-18 22:49 CST

Nmap scan report for scanme.nmap.org (74.207.244.221)
Host is up (0.087s latency).
Not shown: 990 closed ports, 4 filtered ports
PORT      STATE SERVICE
21/tcp    open  ftp
22/tcp    open  ssh
80/tcp    open  http
554/tcp   open  rtsp
7070/tcp  open  realserver
9929/tcp  open  nping-echo

Nmap done: 1 IP address (1 host up) scanned in 7.80 seconds
```

Limiting Nmap output to display open ports only

The --open parameter removes closed and filtered ports from the scan results. This option is useful when you want to unclutter the results of your scan so that only open ports are displayed. The same scan without the --open option is displayed below for comparison.

```
$ nmap scanme.nmap.org

Starting Nmap 6.47 ( http://nmap.org ) at 2015-01-18 22:49 CST

Nmap scan report for scanme.nmap.org (74.207.244.221)
Host is up (0.080s latency).
Not shown: 990 closed ports
PORT      STATE    SERVICE
21/tcp    open     ftp
22/tcp    open     ssh
25/tcp    filtered smtp
80/tcp    open     http
135/tcp   filtered msrpc
139/tcp   filtered netbios-ssn
445/tcp   filtered microsoft-ds
554/tcp   open     rtsp
7070/tcp  open     realserver
9929/tcp  open     nping-echo

Nmap done: 1 IP address (1 host up) scanned in 5.71 seconds
```

Nmap scan displaying open and filtered ports

Section 6: Operating System and Service Detection

Overview

One of Nmap's most remarkable (and incredibly useful) features is its ability to detect operating systems and services on remote systems. This feature analyzes responses from scanned targets and attempts to identify the host's operating system and installed software versions.

The process of identifying a target's operating system and software versions is known as TCP/IP fingerprinting. Although it is not an exact science, Nmap developers have taken great care in making TCP/IP fingerprinting an accurate and reliable feature. This chapter will cover the options used to control this feature and also discusses how to troubleshoot version scans and submit TCP/IP fingerprints for inclusion in the Nmap fingerprint database.

Summary of features covered in this section:

-O
Operating System Detection

--osscan-guess
Attempt to Guess an Unknown OS

-sV
Service Version Detection

--version-trace
Troubleshoot Version Scans

Operating System Detection

The -O parameter enables Nmap's operating system detection feature.

Usage syntax: nmap -O [target]

```
# nmap -O 10.10.4.40

Starting Nmap 6.47 ( http://nmap.org ) at 2015-01-15 13:20 CST

Nmap scan report for 10.10.4.40
[...]
MAC Address: 00:60:E0:55:CD:BC (Axiom Technology CO.)
Device type: general purpose
Running: Microsoft Windows XP|2003
OS CPE: cpe:/o:microsoft:windows_xp::sp2
cpe:/o:microsoft:windows_server_2003::sp1
cpe:/o:microsoft:windows_server_2003::sp2
OS details: Microsoft Windows XP SP2 or Windows Server 2003 SP1 or SP2
Network Distance: 1 hop

OS detection performed. Please report any incorrect results at
http://nmap.org/submit/ .

Nmap done: 1 IP address (1 host up) scanned in 6.47 seconds
```

Output of Nmap's operating system detection feature

As demonstrated above, Nmap is (in most cases) able to identify the operating system on a remote target. Operating system detection is performed by analyzing responses from the target for a set of predictable characteristics that can be used to identify the type of OS on the remote system.

If Nmap is unable determine the OS, it will provide an explanation as to why. If conditions are right, Nmap will display a fingerprint for any unknown systems. You can also force Nmap to guess, which will try to find a close match. These scenarios are discussed next in this chapter.

Tip: *In order for OS detection to work properly there must be at least one open and one closed port on the target system. When scanning multiple targets, the --osscan-limit option can be combined with -O to instruct Nmap not to OS scan hosts that do not meet this criteria. The --max-os-tries option can also be used to speed up scanning by specifying the number of tries Nmap makes to identify an operating system before it gives up (the default is 5).*

Submitting TCP/IP Fingerprints

If Nmap is unable to determine the operating system on a target, it will provide a fingerprint that can be submitted to Nmap's OS database at nmap.org/submit/. The example below demonstrates Nmap's output in this scenario.

```
# nmap -O 10.10.4.1

Starting Nmap 6.47 ( http://nmap.org ) at 2015-01-15 13:11 CST

Nmap scan report for 10.10.4.1
Host is up (0.00036s latency).
Not shown: 999 closed ports
PORT   STATE SERVICE
22/tcp open  ssh
MAC Address: 00:13:3B:10:54:0E (Speed Dragon Multimedia Limited)
No exact OS matches for host (If you know what OS is running on it,
see http://nmap.org/submit/ ).
TCP/IP fingerprint:
OS:SCAN(V=6.47%E=4%D=1/15%OT=22%CT=1%CU=37714%PV=Y%DS=1%DC=D%G=Y%M=00
133B%

[...]

OS detection performed. Please report any incorrect results at
http://nmap.org/submit/ .
Nmap done: 1 IP address (1 host up) scanned in 8.68 seconds
```

TCP/IP fingerprint generated by Nmap

The output section labeled TCP/IP fingerprint provides a long string of characters that contains information needed to submit your discovery. By submitting the fingerprint generated and correctly identifying the target system's operating system, you can help improve the accuracy of Nmap's OS detection feature in future releases.

Attempt to Guess an Unknown Operating System

If Nmap is unable to accurately identify the OS, you can force it to guess by using the --osscan-guess option.

Usage syntax: nmap -O --osscan-guess [target]

```
# nmap -O --osscan-guess 10.10.4.1

Starting Nmap 6.47 ( http://nmap.org ) at 2015-01-26 13:05 CST

Nmap scan report for 10.10.4.1
Host is up (0.00043s latency).
Not shown: 999 closed ports
PORT    STATE SERVICE
22/tcp open  ssh
MAC Address: 00:13:3B:10:54:0E (Speed Dragon Multimedia Limited)
Aggressive OS guesses: Netgear DG834G WAP or Western Digital WD TV
media player (96%), Linux 2.6.32 (95%), Linux 2.6.32 - 3.9 (95%),
Linux 3.8 (93%), Linux 3.1 (93%), Linux 3.2 (93%), AXIS 210A or 211
Network Camera (Linux 2.6) (92%), Linux 2.6.26 - 2.6.35 (92%), Linux
2.6.32 - 2.6.35 (92%), Linux 2.6.32 - 3.2 (92%)
No exact OS matches for host (If you know what OS is running on it,
see http://nmap.org/submit/ ).
TCP/IP fingerprint:

[...]

OS detection performed. Please report any incorrect results at
http://nmap.org/submit/ .
Nmap done: 1 IP address (1 host up) scanned in 16.59 seconds
```

Nmap operating system guess output

The example above displays a list of possible matches for the target's operating system. Each guess is listed with a percentage of confidence Nmap has in the supplied match. While Nmap was unable to determine the exact OS on the target, the results indicate it is likely some sort of Linux based system.

Tip: *The --fuzzy option is a synonym that can be used as an easy to remember shortcut for the --osscan-guess feature.*

Service Version Detection

The -sV parameter enables Nmap's service version detection feature.

Usage syntax: nmap -sV [target]

```
# nmap -sV 10.10.4.70

Starting Nmap 6.47 ( http://nmap.org ) at 2015-01-15 13:32 CST
Nmap scan report for 10.10.4.70
Host is up (0.00019s latency).
Not shown: 993 closed ports
PORT       STATE    SERVICE    VERSION
22/tcp     open     ssh        OpenSSH 6.4 (protocol 2.0)
80/tcp     open     http       Jetty 8.1.10.v20130312
443/tcp    open     ssl/http   Jetty 8.1.10.v20130312
513/tcp    filtered login
514/tcp    filtered shell
3260/tcp   open     iscsi?
5432/tcp   open     postgresql PostgreSQL DB 9.1.5 - 9.1.9
MAC Address: 0C:C4:7A:0B:AB:40 (Unknown)

Service detection performed. Please report any incorrect results at
http://nmap.org/submit/ .
Nmap done: 1 IP address (1 host up) scanned in 133.26 seconds
```

Output of Nmap's service version detection feature

The -sV option will attempt to identify the application and version for any open ports it detects. The results of the above scan show the version information for services that Nmap was successfully able to identify.

Note: *Nmap version detection purposely skips some problematic ports (specifically 9100-9107). These ports are associated with network printers and may cause them to print random garbage when probed for version information. This can be overridden by combining the --allports parameter with -sV which instructs Nmap not to exclude any ports from version detection.*

Tip: *The --version-intensity option can be used with a -sV scan to specify the level of intensity for version scans. The default --version-intensity number is 7. Setting a lower intensity like 1 can speed up scans but will miss a number of identifiable services. A high number like 9 will attempt to detect more services, but will take longer to complete.*

Troubleshooting Version Scans

The --version-trace option can be enabled to display verbose version scan activity.

Usage syntax: nmap -sV --version-trace [target]

```
$ nmap -sV --version-trace 10.10.4.1

Starting Nmap 6.47 ( http://nmap.org ) at 2015-01-15 13:36 CST
PORTS: Using top 1000 ports found open (TCP:1000, UDP:0, SCTP:0)
--------------- Timing report ---------------
  hostgroups: min 1, max 100000
  rtt-timeouts: init 1000, min 100, max 10000
  max-scan-delay: TCP 1000, UDP 1000, SCTP 1000
  parallelism: min 0, max 0
  max-retries: 10, host-timeout: 0
  min-rate: 0, max-rate: 0
---------------------------------------------
NSE: Using Lua 5.2.
NSE: Script Arguments seen from CLI:
NSE: Loaded 23 scripts for scanning.
Overall sending rates: 6172.84 packets / s.
mass_rdns: Using DNS server 10.10.4.46
mass_rdns: 0.02s 0/1 [#: 1, OK: 0, NX: 0, DR: 0, SF: 0, TR: 1]
DNS resolution of 1 IPs took 0.02s. Mode: Async [#: 1, OK: 0, NX: 1, DR: 0, SF: 0, TR: 1, CN: 0]
Overall sending rates: 30639.13 packets / s.
NSOCK INFO [0.2680s] nsi_new2(): nsi_new (IOD #1)
NSOCK INFO [0.2690s] nsock_connect_tcp(): TCP connection requested to 10.10.4.1:22 (IOD #1) EID 8
NSOCK INFO [0.2690s] nsock_trace_handler_callback(): Callback: CONNECT SUCCESS for EID 8 [10.10.4.1:22]
Service scan sending probe NULL to 10.10.4.1:22 (tcp)
NSOCK INFO [0.2690s] nsock_read(): Read request from IOD #1 [10.10.4.1:22] (timeout: 6000ms) EID 18
NSOCK INFO [0.2870s] nsock_trace_handler_callback(): Callback: READ SUCCESS for EID 18 [10.10.4.1:22] (41 bytes): SSH-2.0-OpenSSH_6.6.1p1 Ubuntu-2ubuntu2..
Service scan match (Probe NULL matched with NULL line 3072): 10.10.4.1:22 is ssh. Version: |||protocol 2.0|
NSOCK INFO [0.2880s] nsock_read(): Read request from IOD #1 [10.10.4.1:22] (timeout: 5982ms) EID 26
[...]
```

Version scan trace output

The --version-trace option can be helpful for debugging problems or to gain additional information about the target system. When submitting new fingerprints or corrections, the Nmap developers may ask you to provide this information to help improve the version database.

For more information about troubleshooting and debugging Nmap see

Section 10.

Tip: *Combine the | more pager at the end of the command to improve readability when doing version tracing. You can also redirect the output to a file by appending >filename.txt to the end of the command.*

Section 7: Timing Options

Overview

Many Nmap features have configurable timing options. These timing options can be used to speed up or slow down scanning operations depending on your needs. When scanning a large number of hosts on a fast network, you may want to increase the number of parallel operations to get faster results. Alternatively, when scanning slow networks (or across the internet) you may want to throttle a scan to get more accurate results or evade intrusion detection systems. This section discusses Nmap's options available for these timing features.

Summary of features covered in this section:

-T[0-5]
Timing Templates

--ttl
Set the Packet TTL

--min-parallelism
Minimum # of Parallel Operations

--max-parallelism
Maximum # of Parallel Operations

--min-hostgroup
Minimum Host Group Size

--max-hostgroup
Maximum Host Group Size

--max-rtt-timeout
Maximum RTT Timeout

--initial-rtt-timeout
Initial RTT Timeout

--max-retries
Maximum Retries

--host-timeout
Host Timeout

--scan-delay
Minimum Scan Delay

--max-scan-delay
Maximum Scan Delay

--min-rate
Minimum Packet Rate

--max-rate
Maximum Packet Rate

--defeat-rst-ratelimit
Defeat Reset Rate Limits

Timing Parameters

Certain Nmap options accept timing parameters to adjust various thresholds. You can manually specify timing parameters in milliseconds, seconds, minutes, or hours by appending a qualifier to the time argument. The table below provides examples of time parameter usage syntax.

Note: *Nmap timing parameters in Nmap 6 are accepted as seconds by default. Versions 5 and earlier use milliseconds as the default timing parameter.*

Parameter	Definition	Example	Meaning
ms	Milliseconds (1/1000 of a second)	500ms	500 milliseconds
s *or* (none)	Seconds (default)	10	10 seconds
m	Minutes	5m	5 minutes
h	Hours	1h	1 hour

Nmap timing parameters

Take, for example, the --host-timeout option (discussed later in this section) which uses a timing parameter. To specify a five-minute timeout you can use any of the following forms of time specification:

```
nmap --host-timeout 300000ms 10.10.4.1
nmap --host-timeout 300s 10.10.4.1
nmap --host-timeout 300 10.10.4.1
nmap --host-timeout 5m 10.10.4.1
```

Since 300000 milliseconds and 300 seconds both equal 5 minutes, any of the above commands will produce the same result.

Timing Templates

The -T parameter is used to specify a timing template for an Nmap scan.

Usage syntax: nmap -T[0-5] [target]

```
$ nmap -T4 10.10.4.26

Starting Nmap 6.47 ( http://nmap.org ) at 2015-01-15 15:44 CST
Nmap scan report for 10.10.4.26
Host is up (0.0013s latency).
Not shown: 994 closed ports
PORT     STATE SERVICE
21/tcp   open  ftp
22/tcp   open  ssh
25/tcp   open  smtp
80/tcp   open  http
111/tcp  open  rpcbind
443/tcp  open  https

Nmap done: 1 IP address (1 host up) scanned in 0.17 seconds
```

Using a timing template

Timing templates are handy shortcuts for various timing options (discussed later in this section). There are six templates (numbered 0-5) that can be used to speed up scanning (for faster results) or to slow down scanning (to evade firewalls). The table below describes each timing template.

Template	Name	Notes
-T0	paranoid	Extremely slow
-T1	sneaky	Useful for avoiding intrusion detection systems
-T2	polite	Unlikely to interfere with the target system
-T3	normal	This is the default timing template
-T4	aggressive	Produces faster results on speedy networks
-T5	insane	Extremely fast and aggressive scan

Nmap timing templates

Minimum Number of Parallel Operations

The --min-parallelism option is used to specify the minimum number of parallel port scan operations Nmap should perform at any given time.

Usage syntax: nmap --min-parallelism [number] [target]

```
# nmap --min-parallelism 100 10.10.4.100-200

Starting Nmap 6.47 ( http://nmap.org ) at 2015-01-15 15:47 CST
Nmap scan report for 10.10.4.102
Host is up (0.0016s latency).
All 1000 scanned ports on 10.10.4.102 are closed

Nmap scan report for 10.10.4.104
Host is up (0.0013s latency).
All 1000 scanned ports on 10.10.4.104 are closed (932) or filtered (68)

[...]

Nmap done: 101 IP addresses (23 hosts up) scanned in 15.49 seconds
```

Specifying the minimum number of parallel operations

Nmap automatically adjusts parallel scanning options based on network conditions. In some cases, you may want to specify your own custom setting. The above example instructs Nmap to always perform at least 100 parallel operations at any given time.

Note: *While manually setting the --min-parallelism option may increase scan performance; setting it too high may produce inaccurate results.*

Maximum Number of Parallel Operations

The --max-parallelism option is used to control the maximum number of parallel port scan operations Nmap will perform at any given time.

Usage syntax: nmap --max-parallelism [number] [target]

```
# nmap --max-parallelism 1 scanme.nmap.org

Starting Nmap 6.47 ( http://nmap.org ) at 2015-01-15 15:52 CST
Nmap scan report for scanme.nmap.org (74.207.244.221)
Host is up (0.058s latency).
Not shown: 997 closed ports
PORT      STATE SERVICE
22/tcp    open  ssh
80/tcp    open  http
9929/tcp  open  nping-echo

Nmap done: 1 IP address (1 host up) scanned in 58.61 seconds
```

Specifying the maximum number of parallel operations

In the above example, --max-parallelism 1 is used to restrict Nmap so that only one operation is performed at a time. This scan will be considerably slow, but will be less likely to overwhelm the target system with a flood of packets. This can help prevent triggering red flags with intrusion detection systems.

Minimum Host Group Size

The --min-hostgroup option is used to specify the minimum number of targets Nmap should scan in parallel.

Usage syntax: nmap --min-hostgroup [number] [targets]

```
# nmap --min-hostgroup 30 10.10.4.0/24

Starting Nmap 6.47 ( http://nmap.org ) at 2015-01-15 15:56 CST
Nmap scan report for 10.10.4.1
Host is up (0.00021s latency).
Not shown: 999 closed ports
PORT    STATE SERVICE
22/tcp  open  ssh

Nmap scan report for 10.10.4.2
Host is up (0.00064s latency).
Not shown: 988 closed ports
PORT     STATE SERVICE
21/tcp   open  ftp
135/tcp  open  msrpc
139/tcp  open  netbios-ssn
445/tcp  open  microsoft-ds
[...]
Nmap done: 256 IP addresses (66 hosts up) scanned in 34.26 seconds
```

Specifying a minimum host group size

Nmap will perform scans in parallel to save time when scanning multiple targets such as a range or entire subnet. By default, Nmap will automatically adjust the size of the host groups based on the type of scan being performed and network conditions. By specifying the --min-hostgroup option, Nmap will attempt to keep the group sizes above the specified number.

Maximum Host Group Size

The --max-hostgroup option is used to specify the maximum number of targets Nmap should scan in parallel.

Usage syntax: nmap --max-hostgroup [number] [targets]

```
# nmap --max-hostgroup 10 10.10.4.0/24

Starting Nmap 6.47 ( http://nmap.org ) at 2015-01-15 15:58 CST
Nmap scan report for 10.10.4.1
Host is up (0.00017s latency).
Not shown: 999 closed ports
PORT   STATE SERVICE
22/tcp open  ssh

Nmap scan report for 10.10.4.2
Host is up (0.0017s latency).
Not shown: 988 closed ports
PORT     STATE SERVICE
21/tcp   open  ftp
135/tcp  open  msrpc
139/tcp  open  netbios-ssn
445/tcp  open  microsoft-ds
[...]

Nmap done: 256 IP addresses (66 hosts up) scanned in 67.01 seconds
```

Specifying a maximum host group size

In contrast to the --min-hostgroup option, the --max-hostgroup option controls the maximum number of hosts in a group. This option is helpful if you want to reduce the load on a network or to avoid triggering any red flags with various network security systems.

Initial RTT Timeout

The --initial-rtt-timeout option controls the initial RTT (round-trip time) timeout value used by Nmap.

Usage syntax: nmap --initial-rtt-timeout [time] [target]

```
# nmap --initial-rtt-timeout 5s scanme.nmap.org

Starting Nmap 6.40 ( http://nmap.org ) at 2015-02-08 16:00 CST
Nmap scan report for scanme.nmap.org (74.207.244.221)
Host is up (0.29s latency).
Not shown: 997 closed ports
PORT      STATE SERVICE
22/tcp    open  ssh
80/tcp    open  http
9929/tcp  open  nping-echo

Nmap done: 1 IP address (1 host up) scanned in 1.06 seconds
```

Specifying the initial RTT timeout value used by Nmap

The default timing template has an --initial-rtt-timeout value of 1000 milliseconds. Increasing the value will reduce the number of packet retransmissions due to timeouts. By decreasing the value you can speed up scans – but do so with caution. Setting the RTT timeout value too low can negate any potential performance gains and lead to inaccurate results.

Maximum RTT Timeout

The --max-rtt-timeout option is used to specify the maximum RTT (round-trip time) timeout for a packet response.

Usage syntax: nmap --max-rtt-timeout [time] [target]

```
# nmap --max-rtt-timeout 400ms scanme.nmap.org

Starting Nmap 6.47 ( http://nmap.org ) at 2015-01-21 15:10 CST
Nmap scan report for scanme.nmap.org (74.207.244.221)
Host is up (0.17s latency).
Not shown: 997 closed ports
PORT      STATE SERVICE
22/tcp    open  ssh
80/tcp    open  http
9929/tcp  open  nping-echo

Nmap done: 1 IP address (1 host up) scanned in 4.93 seconds
```

Specifying a 400 millisecond maximum RTT timeout

Nmap dynamically adjusts RTT timeout options for best results by default. The default maximum RTT timeout is 10 seconds. Manually adjusting the maximum RTT timeout lower will allow for faster scan times (especially when scanning large blocks of addresses). Specifying a high maximum RTT timeout will prevent Nmap from giving up too soon when scanning over slow/unreliable connections. Typical values are between 100 milliseconds for fast/reliable networks and 10000 milliseconds for slow/unreliable connections.

Maximum Retries

The --max-retries option is used to control the maximum number of probe retransmissions Nmap will attempt to perform.

Usage syntax: nmap --max-retries [number] [target]

```
# nmap --max-retries 2 scanme.nmap.org

Starting Nmap 6.47 ( http://nmap.org ) at 2015-01-21 15:14 CST
Nmap scan report for scanme.nmap.org (74.207.244.221)
Host is up (0.12s latency).
Not shown: 997 closed ports
PORT      STATE SERVICE
22/tcp    open  ssh
80/tcp    open  http
9929/tcp  open  nping-echo

Nmap done: 1 IP address (1 host up) scanned in 4.52 seconds
```

Specifying the maximum number of retries

By default, Nmap will automatically adjust the number of probe retransmissions based on network conditions. The --max-retries option can be used if you want to override the default settings or troubleshoot a connectivity problem. Specifying a high number can increase the time it takes for a scan to complete, but will produce more accurate results. By lowering the --max-retries you can speed up a scan – although you may not get accurate results if Nmap gives up too quickly.

Set the Packet TTL

The --ttl option is used to specify the IP TTL (time-to-live) for the specified scan (in seconds/hops).

Usage syntax: nmap --ttl [0-256] [target]

```
# nmap --ttl 20 scanme.nmap.org

Starting Nmap 6.47 ( http://nmap.org ) at 2015-01-21 15:13 CST
Nmap scan report for scanme.nmap.org (74.207.244.221)
Host is up (0.11s latency).
Not shown: 997 closed ports
PORT     STATE SERVICE
22/tcp   open  ssh
80/tcp   open  http
9929/tcp open  nping-echo

Nmap done: 1 IP address (1 host up) scanned in 4.53 seconds
```

Specifying a TTL parameter of 20

Packets sent using this option will have the specified TTL value. This option is useful when scanning targets on slow/distant connections where normal packets may time out before receiving a response. The TTL is specified in seconds, but each hop decreases the value by at least 1 regardless of the amount of time elapsed. Therefore, the TTL can also be referred to as a hop limit.

Host Timeout

The --host-timeout option causes Nmap to give up on slow hosts after the specified time.

Usage syntax: nmap --host-timeout [time] [target]

```
$ nmap --host-timeout 500ms scanme.nmap.org

Starting Nmap 6.47 ( http://nmap.org ) at 2015-01-15 16:19 CST
Nmap scan report for scanme.nmap.org (74.207.244.221)
Host is up (0.059s latency).
Skipping host scanme.nmap.org (74.207.244.221) due to host timeout
Nmap done: 1 IP address (1 host up) scanned in 0.58 seconds
```

Output of an Nmap scan when specifying a short host timeout

A host may take a long time to scan if it is located on a slow or unreliable network. Systems that are protected by rate limiting firewalls may also take a considerable amount of time to scan. The --host-timeout option instructs Nmap to give up on the target system if it fails to complete after the specified time interval. In the above example, the scan takes longer than 500 milliseconds to complete (as specified by the 500ms parameter) which causes Nmap to terminate the scan. This is an unrealistic host timeout option, but it can be particularly useful in other scenarios. One example is when scanning multiple systems across a WAN or internet connection where you don't mind waiting for slow systems to get better results. Another is when trying to do a quick scan on a large number of hosts when accuracy isn't a priority.

Note: *Nmap performs parallel operations when scanning multiple targets. In the event that one host is taking a long time to respond, Nmap is likely scanning other hosts during that time. This reduces potential bottlenecks that slow hosts can create.*

Warning: *When the --host-timeout option is specified, Nmap will not display any results if a host exceeds the timeout (even if it discovered open ports).*

Minimum Scan Delay

The --scan-delay option instructs Nmap to pause for the specified time interval between probes.

Usage syntax: nmap --scan-delay [time] [target]

```
# nmap --scan-delay 1s -F 10.10.3.1

Starting Nmap 6.47 ( http://nmap.org ) at 2015-01-15 16:36 CST
Nmap scan report for 10.10.3.1
Host is up (0.00080s latency).
Not shown: 97 closed ports
PORT     STATE SERVICE
22/tcp   open  ssh
80/tcp   open  http
443/tcp  open  https

Nmap done: 1 IP address (1 host up) scanned in 101.17 seconds
```

Specifying a 1 second minimum scan delay

Nmap attempts to strike a balance between performance and reliability when sending probes. Some systems employ rate limiting which can hamper Nmap scanning attempts. Nmap will automatically adjust the scan delay by default on systems where rate limiting is detected. In some cases it may be useful to specify your own scan delay if you know that rate limiting or IDS (Intrusion Detection Systems) are in use. In the example above, the scan delay of 1s instructs Nmap to wait one second between probes. This can take a considerable amount of time but helps prevent triggering any red flags.

Maximum Scan Delay

The --max-scan-delay is used to specify the maximum amount of time Nmap should wait between probes.

Usage syntax: nmap --max-scan-delay [time] [target]

```
# nmap --max-scan-delay 50ms 10.10.3.1

Starting Nmap 6.47 ( http://nmap.org ) at 2015-01-15 16:39 CST
Nmap scan report for 10.10.3.1
Host is up (0.072s latency).
Not shown: 997 closed ports
PORT     STATE SERVICE
22/tcp   open  ssh
80/tcp   open  http
443/tcp  open  https

Nmap done: 1 IP address (1 host up) scanned in 0.60 seconds
```

Specifying a 50 millisecond maximum scan delay

Nmap automatically adjusts the scan delay to accommodate network conditions and/or rate limiting hosts. The --max-scan-delay option can be used to provide an upper limit to the amount of time between probes. This can speed up a scan, but comes at the expense of accurate results and added network stress. In the example above, a 50 millisecond scan delay is specified. This causes Nmap to wait a maximum of 50ms between probes.

Minimum Packet Rate

The --min-rate option is used to specify the minimum number of packets Nmap should send per second.

Usage syntax: nmap --min-rate [number] [target]

```
$ nmap --min-rate 30 scanme.nmap.org

Starting Nmap 6.47 ( http://nmap.org ) at 2015-01-17 10:54 CST
Nmap scan report for scanme.nmap.org (74.207.244.221)
Host is up (0.056s latency).
Not shown: 997 closed ports
PORT      STATE SERVICE
22/tcp    open  ssh
80/tcp    open  http
9929/tcp  open  nping-echo

Nmap done: 1 IP address (1 host up) scanned in 1.07 seconds
```

Specifying a minimum packet transmission rate of 30

Nmap, by default, will automatically adjust the packet rate for a scan based on network conditions. In some cases you may want to specify your own minimum rate - although this is generally not necessary. In the above example --min-rate 30 instructs Nmap to send at least 30 packets per second. Nmap will use the number as a low threshold but may scan faster than this if network conditions allow.

Warning: *Setting the --min-rate too high may reduce the accuracy of a scan.*

Maximum Packet Rate

The --max-rate option specifies the maximum number of packets Nmap should send per second.

Usage syntax: nmap --max-rate [number] [target]

```
$ nmap --max-rate 30 scanme.nmap.org

Starting Nmap 6.47 ( http://nmap.org ) at 2015-01-17 10:54 CST
Nmap scan report for scanme.nmap.org (74.207.244.221)
Host is up (0.055s latency).
Not shown: 997 closed ports
PORT      STATE SERVICE
22/tcp    open  ssh
80/tcp    open  http
9929/tcp  open  nping-echo

Nmap done: 1 IP address (1 host up) scanned in 33.58 seconds
```

Using a maximum packet transmission rate of 30

In the example above, specifying --max-rate 30 instructs Nmap to send no more than 30 packets per second. This can dramatically slow down a scan but can be helpful when attempting to avoid intrusion detection systems or a target that uses rate limiting.

Tip: *To perform a very sneaky scan use --max-rate 0.1 which instructs Nmap to send one packet every ten seconds.*

Defeat Reset Rate Limits

The --defeat-rst-ratelimit is used to defeat targets that apply rate limiting to RST (reset) packets.

Usage syntax: nmap --defeat-rst-ratelimit [target]

```
# nmap --defeat-rst-ratelimit scanme.nmap.org

Starting Nmap 6.47 ( http://nmap.org ) at 2015-01-17 10:56 CST
Nmap scan report for scanme.nmap.org (74.207.244.221)
Host is up (0.20s latency).
Not shown: 997 closed ports
PORT      STATE SERVICE
22/tcp    open  ssh
80/tcp    open  http
9929/tcp  open  nping-echo

Nmap done: 1 IP address (1 host up) scanned in 4.36 seconds
```

Defeating RST rate limits

The --defeat-rst-ratelimit option can be useful if you want to speed up scans on targets that implement RST packet rate limits. It can, however, lead to inaccurate results and as such is rarely used.

Note: *The --defeat-rst-ratelimit option is rarely used because, in most cases, Nmap will automatically detect rate limiting hosts and adjust itself accordingly.*

Section 8: Evading Firewalls

Overview

Firewalls and intrusion prevention systems are designed to prevent tools like Nmap from getting an accurate picture of the systems they are protecting. Nmap includes a number of features designed to circumvent these defenses. This section discusses the various evasion techniques built into Nmap.

Summary of features covered in this section:

-f
Fragment Packets

--mtu
Specify a Specific MTU

-D
Use a Decoy

-sI
Idle Zombie Scan

--source-port
Manually Specify a Source Port

--data-length
Append Random Data

--randomize-hosts
Randomize Target Scan Order

--spoof-mac
Spoof MAC Address

--badsum
Send Bad Checksums

Fragment Packets

The -f option is used to fragment probes into 8-byte packets.

Usage syntax: nmap -f [target]

```
# nmap -f 10.10.4.26

Starting Nmap 6.47 ( http://nmap.org ) at 2015-01-17 10:59 CST
Nmap scan report for 10.10.4.26
Host is up (0.000024s latency).
Not shown: 994 closed ports
PORT     STATE SERVICE
21/tcp   open  ftp
22/tcp   open  ssh
25/tcp   open  smtp
80/tcp   open  http
111/tcp  open  rpcbind
443/tcp  open  https

Nmap done: 1 IP address (1 host up) scanned in 2.35 seconds
```

Scanning a target using fragmented packets

The -f option instructs Nmap to send small 8-byte packets thus fragmenting the probe into many very small packets. This option isn't particularly useful in everyday situations. It may be helpful, however, when attempting to evade some older or improperly configured firewalls.

Tip: *Some host operating systems may require the use of --send-eth combined with -f for fragmented packets to be properly transmitted.*

Specify a Specific MTU

The --mtu option is used to specify a custom MTU (Maximum Transmission Unit).

Usage syntax: nmap --mtu [number] [target]

```
# nmap --mtu 16 10.10.4.26

Starting Nmap 6.47 ( http://nmap.org ) at 2015-01-17 11:00 CST
Nmap scan report for 10.10.4.26
Host is up (0.000019s latency).
Not shown: 994 closed ports
PORT     STATE SERVICE
21/tcp   open  ftp
22/tcp   open  ssh
25/tcp   open  smtp
80/tcp   open  http
111/tcp  open  rpcbind
443/tcp  open  https

Nmap done: 1 IP address (1 host up) scanned in 2.35 seconds
```

Specifying a specific MTU

The --mtu option is similar to the -f option except it allows you to specify your own MTU to be used during scanning. This creates fragmented packets that can potentially confuse some firewalls. In the above example, the --mtu 16 argument instructs Nmap to use tiny 16-byte packets for the scan.

Note: *The MTU must be a multiple of 8 (example 8, 16, 24, 32, etc).*

Tip: *Some host operating systems may require the use of --send-eth combined with --mtu for fragmented packets to be properly transmitted.*

Use a Decoy

The -D option can be used to mask an Nmap scan by creating one or more decoys.

Usage syntax: nmap -D [decoy1,decoy2,etc|RND:number] [target]

```
# nmap -D RND:10 10.10.3.1

Starting Nmap 6.47 ( http://nmap.org ) at 2015-01-17 11:05 CST
Nmap scan report for 10.10.3.1
Host is up (0.00073s latency).
Not shown: 997 closed ports
PORT     STATE SERVICE
22/tcp   open  ssh
80/tcp   open  http
443/tcp  open  https

Nmap done: 1 IP address (1 host up) scanned in 52.56 seconds
```

Masking a scan using 10 randomly generated decoy IP addresses

When performing a decoy scan, Nmap will spoof additional packets from the specified number of decoy addresses. This effectively makes it appear that the target is being scanned by multiple systems simultaneously. Using decoys allows the actual source of the scan to "blend into the crowd" which makes it harder to trace where the scan is coming from.

In the above example, nmap -D RND:10 instructs Nmap to generate 10 random decoys. You can also specify decoy addresses manually using the following syntax: nmap -D decoy1,decoy2,decoy3,etc.

Warning: *Using too many decoys can cause network congestion and reduce the effectiveness of a scan. Additionally, some systems may be configured to filter spoofed traffic which will reduce the effectiveness of using decoys to cloak your scanning activity.*

Idle Zombie Scan

The -sI option is used to perform an idle zombie scan.

Usage syntax: nmap -sI [zombie host] [target]

```
# nmap -Pn -sI 10.10.4.44 10.10.4.26

Starting Nmap 6.47 ( http://nmap.org ) at 2015-01-17 11:13 CST

Idle scan using zombie 10.10.4.44 (10.10.4.44:80); Class: Incremental
Nmap scan report for 10.10.4.26
Host is up (0.049s latency).
Not shown: 994 closed|filtered ports
PORT     STATE SERVICE
21/tcp   open  ftp
22/tcp   open  ssh
25/tcp   open  smtp
80/tcp   open  http
111/tcp  open  rpcbind
443/tcp  open  https
MAC Address: 00:50:56:BA:28:6F (VMware)

Nmap done: 1 IP address (1 host up) scanned in 6.99 seconds
```

Using an idle "zombie" to scan a target

The idle zombie scan is a unique scanning technique that allows you to exploit an idle system and use it to scan a target system for you. In this example 10.10.4.44 is the zombie and 10.10.4.26 is the target system. This scan works by exploiting the predictable IP sequence ID generation employed by some systems. In order for an idle scan to be successful, the zombie system must truly be idle at the time of scanning.

Tip: *Idle network printers make great zombies.*

Note: *With this scan no probe packets are sent from your system to the target, although an initial ping packet will be sent to the target unless you combine -Pn with -sI.*

Manually Specify a Source Port Number

The --source-port option is used to manually specify the source port number of a probe.

Usage syntax: nmap --source-port [port] [target]

```
# nmap --source-port 53 scanme.nmap.org

Starting Nmap 6.47 ( http://nmap.org ) at 2015-01-17 11:14 CST
Nmap scan report for scanme.nmap.org (74.207.244.221)
Host is up (0.24s latency).
Not shown: 997 closed ports
PORT      STATE SERVICE
22/tcp    open  ssh
80/tcp    open  http
9929/tcp  open  nping-echo

Nmap done: 1 IP address (1 host up) scanned in 4.21 seconds
```

Manually specifying the packet source port number

Every TCP segment contains a source port number in addition to a destination. By default, Nmap will randomly pick an available outgoing source port to probe a target. The --source-port option will force Nmap to use the specified port as the source for all packets. This technique can be used to exploit weaknesses in firewalls that are improperly configured to blindly accept incoming traffic based on a specific port number. Port 20 (FTP), 53 (DNS), and 67 (DHCP) are common ports susceptible to this type of scan.

Tip: *The -g option is a shortcut that is synonymous with --source-port.*

Append Random Data

The --data-length option can be used to append random data to probe packets.

Usage syntax: nmap --data-length [number] [target]

```
# nmap --data-length 25 10.10.3.1

Starting Nmap 6.47 ( http://nmap.org ) at 2015-01-17 11:15 CST
Nmap scan report for 10.10.3.1
Host is up (0.17s latency).
Not shown: 997 closed ports
PORT    STATE SERVICE
22/tcp  open  ssh
80/tcp  open  http
443/tcp open  https

Nmap done: 1 IP address (1 host up) scanned in 7.16 seconds
```

Padding a scan with random data

Nmap normally sends empty packets when performing a port scan. The --data-length option adds the specified amount of random data as a payload each packet. This can occasionally produce a response where an empty packet might not. In the above example 25-bytes are added to all packets sent to the target.

Note: *Payloads larger than 1400 are larger than many systems' MTU and may not be sent successfully. Nmap will allow you to attempt this, but will display a warning message for any value above 1400.*

Randomize Target Scan Order

The --randomize-hosts option is used to randomize the scanning order of the specified targets.

Usage syntax: nmap --randomize-hosts [targets]

```
$ nmap -F --randomize-hosts 10.10.4.1-50

Starting Nmap 6.47 ( http://nmap.org ) at 2015-01-17 11:19 CST
Nmap scan report for 10.10.4.34
Host is up (0.0026s latency).
Not shown: 98 closed ports
PORT     STATE SERVICE
22/tcp   open  ssh
443/tcp  open  https

Nmap scan report for 10.10.4.15
Host is up (0.00078s latency).
Not shown: 98 closed ports
PORT     STATE SERVICE
80/tcp   open  http
443/tcp  open  https

Nmap scan report for 10.10.4.25
Host is up (0.00034s latency).
Not shown: 98 closed ports
PORT     STATE SERVICE
22/tcp open   ssh
25/tcp open   smtp

Nmap scan report for 10.10.4.21
Host is up (0.0033s latency).
Not shown: 97 closed ports
PORT     STATE SERVICE
21/tcp open   ftp
[...]
```

Scanning systems in a random order

The --randomize-hosts option can help prevent scans of multiple targets behind the same firewall from being detected by intrusion detection algorithms. This is done by scanning them in a random order instead of sequential. Combining this technique with the previously discussed timing options can further help prevent tripping any alarms.

Spoof MAC Address

The --spoof-mac option is used to spoof the MAC (Media Access Control) address of an ethernet device.

Usage syntax: nmap --spoof-mac [vendor|MAC|0] [target]

```
$ nmap -PN --spoof-mac 0 10.10.4.26

Starting Nmap 6.47 ( http://nmap.org ) at 2015-01-17 11:22 CST
Spoofing MAC address 3F:54:1A:60:BF:B9 (No registered vendor)
Nmap scan report for 10.10.4.26
Host is up (0.0013s latency).
Not shown: 994 closed ports
PORT     STATE SERVICE
21/tcp   open  ftp
22/tcp   open  ssh
25/tcp   open  smtp
80/tcp   open  http
111/tcp  open  rpcbind
443/tcp  open  https

Nmap done: 1 IP address (1 host up) scanned in 0.16 seconds
```

Using a spoofed MAC address

In this example, Nmap is instructed to forge a randomly generated MAC address. This makes your scanning activity harder to trace by preventing your real MAC address from being logged while scanning the target.

The --spoof-mac option can be controlled by the following parameters:

0 (zero)
Generates a random MAC address

Specific MAC Address
Uses the specified MAC address

Vendor Name
Generates a MAC address from the specified vendor (such as Apple, Dell, 3Com, etc)

133

Send Bad Checksums

The --badsum option is used to send packets with incorrect checksums to the specified host.

Usage syntax: nmap --badsum [target]

```
# nmap --badsum 10.10.4.1

Starting Nmap 6.47 ( http://nmap.org ) at 2015-01-17 11:25 CST
Nmap scan report for 10.10.4.1
Host is up (0.00043s latency).
All 1000 scanned ports on 10.10.4.1 are filtered
MAC Address: 00:13:3B:10:54:0E (Speed Dragon Multimedia Limited)

Nmap done: 1 IP address (1 host up) scanned in 21.36 seconds
```

Scanning a target using bad checksums

TCP and UDP use checksums to ensure data integrity. Crafting packets with bad checksums can, in some rare occasions, produce a response from a poorly designed system. In the above example we did not receive any results, meaning the target system adheres correctly to the TCP protocol. This is a typical result when using the --badsum option.

Note: *Only a poorly designed system would respond to a packet with a bad checksum. Nevertheless, it is a good tool to use when auditing network security or attempting to evade firewalls.*

Section 9: Output Options

Overview

Nmap offers several options for creating formatted output. In addition to displaying the standard output on a screen, you can also save scan results in a text file, XML file, or a single line "grep-able" file. This feature can be helpful when scanning a large number of systems or for comparing the results of two scans using the ndiff utility (discussed in Section 13).

Summary of features covered in this section:

-oN
Save Output to a Text File

-oX
Save Output to a XML File

-oG
Grepable Output

-oA
Output All Supported File Types

-oS
133t Output

Save Output to a Text File

The -oN parameter saves the results of a scan in a plain text file.

Usage syntax: nmap -oN [scan.txt] [target]

```
# nmap -oN scan.txt 10.10.4.1

Starting Nmap 6.47 ( http://nmap.org ) at 2015-01-17 11:27 CST
Nmap scan report for 10.10.4.1
Host is up (0.00016s latency).
Not shown: 999 closed ports
PORT   STATE SERVICE
22/tcp open  ssh
MAC Address: 00:13:3B:10:54:0E (Speed Dragon Multimedia Limited)

Nmap done: 1 IP address (1 host up) scanned in 1.69 seconds
```

Saving Nmap output in a text file

The results of the above scan are saved to the scan.txt file shown below.

```
$ cat scan.txt
# Nmap 6.47 scan initiated Sat Jan 17 11:27:36 2015 as: nmap -oN scan.txt 10.10.4.1
Nmap scan report for 10.10.4.1
Host is up (0.00016s latency).
Not shown: 999 closed ports
PORT   STATE SERVICE
22/tcp open  ssh
MAC Address: 00:13:3B:10:54:0E (Speed Dragon Multimedia Limited)

# Nmap done at Sat Jan 17 11:27:37 2015 -- 1 IP address (1 host up) scanned in 1.69 seconds
```

Reviewing the contents of the scan.txt file

Note: *Nmap will overwrite an existing output file unless the --append-output option is combined with -oN.*

Save Output to a XML File

The -oX parameter saves the results of a scan in a XML file.

Usage syntax: nmap -oX [scan.xml] [target]

```
# nmap -oX scan.xml 10.10.4.1

Starting Nmap 6.47 ( http://nmap.org ) at 2015-01-17 11:28 CST
Nmap scan report for 10.10.4.1
Host is up (0.00015s latency).
Not shown: 999 closed ports
PORT    STATE SERVICE
22/tcp  open  ssh
MAC Address: 00:13:3B:10:54:0E (Speed Dragon Multimedia Limited)

Nmap done: 1 IP address (1 host up) scanned in 1.69 seconds
```

Creating a XML output file

The results of the above scan are saved to the scan.xml file shown below.

```
$ cat scan.xml
<?xml version="1.0"?>
<?xml-stylesheet href="file:///usr/bin/../share/nmap/nmap.xsl"
type="text/xsl"?>
<!-- Nmap 6.47 scan initiated Sat Jan 17 11:28:48 2015 as: nmap -oX
scan.xml 10.10.4.1 -->
<nmaprun scanner="nmap" args="nmap -oX scan.xml 10.10.4.1"
start="1421515728" startstr="Sat Jan 17 11:28:48 2015" version="6.47"
xmloutputversion="1.04">
[...]
```

Viewing the contents of the XML output file

Note: *The resulting XML file has hardcoded file paths which may only work on the system where the file was created. The --webxml parameter can be combined with -oX to create a portable file for any system (with internet access). To avoid referencing a style sheet at all, use the --no-stylesheet parameter.*

Grepable Output

The -oG option enables grepable output.

Usage syntax: nmap -oG [scan.txt] [target]

```
# nmap -oG scan.txt -F -O 10.10.4.1/24

Starting Nmap 6.47 ( http://nmap.org ) at 2015-01-21 12:10 CST
[...]
```

Creating a grepable output file

The -oG option produces single-line output that is easy to filter using tools like the Unix/Linux grep utility. The example below demonstrates using grep to search for all results matching the quoted text.

```
# grep "Windows Server 2003" scan.txt
Host: 10.10.4.40 ()       Ports: 21/open/tcp//ftp///,
25/open/tcp//smtp///, 80/open/tcp//http///, 135/open/tcp//msrpc///,
139/open/tcp//netbios-ssn///, 143/open/tcp//imap///,
443/open/tcp//https///, 445/open/tcp//microsoft-ds///,
1025/open/tcp//NFS-or-IIS///, 1026/open/tcp//LSA-or-nterm///,
1028/open/tcp//unknown///, 3389/open/tcp//ms-wbt-server///,
7070/open/tcp//realserver///       Ignored State: closed (87) OS:
Microsoft Windows Server 2003 SP1 or SP2|Microsoft Windows XP SP2 or
Windows Server 2003 SP1 or SP2    Seq Index: 244   IP ID Seq: Busy
server or unknown class
[...]
```

Using the grep utility to review an Nmap output file

In the above example, the grep utility will display all instances of the specified text found in the scan.txt file. This makes it simple to quickly search for specific information when analyzing results from a large scan.

Note: *The grep pattern matching utility is only available on Unix, Linux, and Mac OS X systems by default. Windows users can download a Win32 port of the GNU grep program at gnuwin32.sourceforge.net to use with the examples discussed in this section.*

Output All Supported File Types

The -oA parameter saves the output of a scan in text, grepable, and XML formats.

Usage syntax: nmap -oA [filename] [target]

```
$ nmap -oA scans 10.10.3.1

Starting Nmap 6.47 ( http://nmap.org ) at 2015-01-17 11:41 CST
Nmap scan report for 10.10.3.1
Host is up (0.20s latency).
Not shown: 997 closed ports
PORT     STATE SERVICE
22/tcp   open  ssh
80/tcp   open  http
443/tcp  open  https

Nmap done: 1 IP address (1 host up) scanned in 3.72 seconds
```

Creating output files for all available formats

The resulting scan's output files are created with their respective extensions as displayed below.

```
$ ls -l scans.*
-rw-r--r-- 1 root root  323 Jan 17 11:41 scans.gnmap
-rw-r--r-- 1 root root  340 Jan 17 11:41 scans.nmap
-rw-r--r-- 1 root root 5295 Jan 17 11:41 scans.xml
```

Directory listing of the resulting output files

Nmap output files:

scans.gnmap
Grepable output

scans.nmap
Plain text output

scans.xml
XML output

133t Output

The -oS option enables "script kiddie" output.

Usage syntax: nmap -oS [scan.txt] [target]

```
$ nmap -oS scan.txt 10.10.3.1

Starting Nmap 6.47 ( http://nmap.org ) at 2015-01-17 11:45 CST
Nmap scan report for 10.10.3.1
Host is up (0.15s latency).
Not shown: 997 closed ports
PORT     STATE SERVICE
22/tcp   open  ssh
80/tcp   open  http
443/tcp  open  https

Nmap done: 1 IP address (1 host up) scanned in 4.17 seconds
```

Creating a "133t" output file

Script kiddie or "leet" speak output is a cryptic form of typing used mostly by immature teenagers on message boards and chat sites. This option is included as a joke and isn't really useful for anything other than a good laugh and proving that the Nmap developers have a good sense of humor. The results of the -oS option are saved in the scan.txt file displayed below.

```
$ cat scan.txt

Start|Ng NmaP 6.47 ( hTtp://nmAp.org ) at 2015-01-17 11:45 c$T
nmap scan r3port f0R 10.10.3.1
H0$t is uP (0.15s lateNcy).
Not sh0wn: 997 Clo$ed port$
PORT     $T4TE $3RVIc3
22/tcp   Open  $$h
80/tcp   oPeN  http
443/tcP  OPeN  HtTPz

Nmap don3: 1 1P addr3Sz (1 h0st up) scANn3d in 4.17 Sec0ndz
```

Nmap script kiddie output

Section 10: Troubleshooting and Debugging

Overview

Technical problems are an inherent part of using computers. Nmap is no exception. Occasionally a scan may not produce the output you expected. You may receive an error – or you may not receive any output at all. Nmap offers several options for tracing and debugging a scan, which can help identify why this happens. The following section describes these troubleshooting and debugging features.

Summary of features covered in this section:

-h
Getting Help

-V
Display Nmap Version

-v
Verbose Output

-d
Debugging

--reason
Display Port State Reason

--packet-trace
Trace Packets

--iflist
Display Host Networking

-e
Specify a Network Interface

Getting Help

Executing nmap -h will display a summary of available options.

Usage syntax: nmap -h

```
$ nmap -h | more
Nmap 6.47 ( http://nmap.org )
Usage: nmap [Scan Type(s)] [Options] {target specification}
TARGET SPECIFICATION:
  Can pass hostnames, IP addresses, networks, etc.
  Ex: scanme.nmap.org, microsoft.com/24, 192.168.0.1; 10.0.0-255.1-254
  -iL <inputfilename>: Input from list of hosts/networks
  -iR <num hosts>: Choose random targets
  --exclude <host1[,host2][,host3],...>: Exclude hosts/networks
  --excludefile <exclude_file>: Exclude list from file
[...]
```

Displaying Nmap help information

The -h option displays a quick cheat sheet of Nmap's features. For more detailed information, you can read the Nmap manual page by executing **man nmap** on the command line. The manual for Nmap provides a description of every Nmap feature and is a handy reference when working on the command line.

```
$ man nmap
NMAP(1) Nmap Reference Guide

NAME
nmap - Network exploration tool and security / port scanner

SYNOPSIS
nmap [Scan Type...] [Options] {target specification}

DESCRIPTION
Nmap ("Network Mapper") is an open source tool for network
exploration and [...]
```

Accessing the Nmap man page on Unix and Linux systems

Note: *The man command is only available on Unix, Linux, and Mac OS X based systems. Windows users can read the Nmap manual online at nmap.org/book/man.html.*

Tip: *You can also find help online by subscribing to the Nmap mailing list at seclists.org.*

Display Nmap Version

The -V option (uppercase V) is used to display the installed version of Nmap.

Usage syntax: nmap -V

```
$ nmap -V
Nmap version 6.47 ( http://nmap.org )
Platform: x86_64-pc-linux-gnu
Compiled with: liblua-5.2.3 openssl-1.0.1f libpcre-8.31 libpcap-1.5.3 nmap-libdnet-1.12 ipv6
Compiled without:
Available nsock engines: epoll poll select
```

Displaying the installed version of Nmap

The -V option displays the Nmap version along with other information about how it was compiled. When troubleshooting Nmap problems you should always make sure you have the most up-to-date version installed. Open source programs like Nmap are developed at a rapid pace and critical bugs are typically fixed as soon as they are discovered. Compare your installed version to the latest version available on the Nmap website at nmap.org to make sure you are running the most up-to-date version available. This will ensure that you have access to the latest features as well as the most bug-free version available.

Verbose Output

The -v option (lowercase v) is used to enable verbose output.

Usage syntax: nmap -v [target]

```
# nmap -v scanme.nmap.org

Starting Nmap 6.47 ( http://nmap.org ) at 2015-01-17 11:49 CST
Initiating Ping Scan at 11:49
Scanning scanme.nmap.org (74.207.244.221) [4 ports]
Completed Ping Scan at 11:49, 1.00s elapsed (1 total hosts)
Initiating Parallel DNS resolution of 1 host. at 11:49
Completed Parallel DNS resolution of 1 host. at 11:49, 0.00s elapsed
Initiating SYN Stealth Scan at 11:49
Scanning scanme.nmap.org (74.207.244.221) [1000 ports]
Discovered open port 22/tcp on 74.207.244.221
Discovered open port 80/tcp on 74.207.244.221
Discovered open port 9929/tcp on 74.207.244.221
Completed SYN Stealth Scan at 11:49, 2.00s elapsed (1000 total ports)
Nmap scan report for scanme.nmap.org (74.207.244.221)
Host is up (0.31s latency).
Not shown: 997 closed ports
PORT     STATE SERVICE
22/tcp   open  ssh
80/tcp   open  http
9929/tcp open  nping-echo

Read data files from: /usr/bin/../share/nmap
Nmap done: 1 IP address (1 host up) scanned in 3.09 seconds
          Raw packets sent: 1188 (52.248KB) | Rcvd: 1185 (47.445KB)
```

Nmap scan with verbose output enabled

Verbose output can be useful when troubleshooting connectivity problems, or if you are simply interested in what's going on behind the scenes of your scan. In the example above, verbose output is displayed for the scan in progress. Most of this information appears in real-time, prior to the final port display and summary. Additional information, such as data files and packet counts, is displayed at the end of the scan.

Tip: *You can use -vv to enable additional verbose output.*

Debugging

The -d option enables debugging output.

Usage syntax: nmap -d[1-9] [target]

```
# nmap -d scanme.nmap.org

Starting Nmap 6.47 ( http://nmap.org ) at 2015-01-17 11:49 CST
PORTS: Using top 1000 ports found open (TCP:1000, UDP:0, SCTP:0)
--------------- Timing report ---------------
  hostgroups: min 1, max 100000
  rtt-timeouts: init 1000, min 100, max 10000
  max-scan-delay: TCP 1000, UDP 1000, SCTP 1000
  parallelism: min 0, max 0
  max-retries: 10, host-timeout: 0
  min-rate: 0, max-rate: 0
---------------------------------------------
Initiating Ping Scan at 11:49
Scanning scanme.nmap.org (74.207.244.221) [4 ports]
Packet capture filter (device eth0): dst host 10.10.4.25 and (icmp or
icmp6 or ((tcp or udp or sctp) and (src host 74.207.244.221)))
We got a TCP ping packet back from 74.207.244.221 port 80 (trynum =
0)
Completed Ping Scan at 11:49, 1.00s elapsed (1 total hosts)
Overall sending rates: 3.99 packets / s, 151.48 bytes / s.
mass_rdns: Using DNS server 10.10.4.46
Initiating Parallel DNS resolution of 1 host. at 11:49
mass_rdns: 0.00s 0/1 [#: 1, OK: 0, NX: 0, DR: 0, SF: 0, TR: 1]
Completed Parallel DNS resolution of 1 host. at 11:49, 0.00s elapsed
DNS resolution of 1 IPs took 0.00s. Mode: Async [#: 1, OK: 1, NX: 0,
DR: 0, SF: 0, TR: 1, CN: 0]
Initiating SYN Stealth Scan at 11:49
Scanning scanme.nmap.org (74.207.244.221) [1000 ports]
Packet capture filter (device eth0): dst host 10.10.4.25 and (icmp or
icmp6 or ((tcp or udp or sctp) and (src host 74.207.244.221)))
Discovered open port 22/tcp on 74.207.244.221
Discovered open port 80/tcp on 74.207.244.221
Discovered open port 9929/tcp on 74.207.244.221
Increased max_successful_tryno for 74.207.244.221 to 1 (packet drop)
Completed SYN Stealth Scan at 11:50, 2.00s elapsed (1000 total ports)
Overall sending rates: 501.12 packets / s, 26009.44 bytes / s.
Nmap scan report for scanme.nmap.org (74.207.244.221)
 [...]
```

Nmap debugging output

Debugging output provides additional information that can be used to trace bugs or troubleshoot problems. The default -d output provides a fair amount of debugging information. You can also specify a debugging level of 1-9 to be used with the -d parameter to increase or decrease the amount of output. For example: -d1 provides the lowest amount of debugging output and -d9 is the highest.

Display Port State Reason Codes

The --reason parameter displays the reason why a port is considered to be in the given state.

Usage syntax: nmap --reason [target]

```
# nmap -p25,80,135 --reason 10.10.4.80

Starting Nmap 6.47 ( http://nmap.org ) at 2015-02-08 19:40 CST
Nmap scan report for 10.10.4.80
Host is up, received arp-response (0.00045s latency).
PORT     STATE    SERVICE  REASON
25/tcp   closed   smtp     reset
80/tcp   open     http     syn-ack
135/tcp  filtered msrpc    port-unreach
MAC Address: 00:50:56:BA:F8:B2 (VMware)

Nmap done: 1 IP address (1 host up) scanned in 1.84 seconds
```

Nmap scan with port state reason codes enabled

Notice the addition of the reason field in the above scan. Information in this field can be useful when trying to determine why a target's ports are in a particular state. Ports that respond with syn-ack are considered to be open. Ports that respond with conn-refused or reset are typically closed. Ports that do not respond or at all are generally filtered (by a firewall). An ICMP port unreachable message (port-unreach) is usually the result of a protocol mismatch, but can be generated by numerous other conditions.

Trace Packets

The --packet-trace parameter instructs Nmap to display a summary of all packets sent and received.

Usage syntax: nmap --packet-trace [target]

```
# nmap --packet-trace 10.10.4.1 | more
NSOCK INFO [4.46:53] (timeout: -1ms) EID 34
NSOCK INFO [0.2790s] nsi_delete(): nsi_delete (IOD #1)
NSOCK INFO [0.2790s] msevent_cancel(): msevent_cancel on event #34
(type READ)
SENT (0.2803s) TCP 10.10.4.25:60354 > 10.10.4.1:554 S ttl=50 id=6247
iplen=44  seq=1617903748 win=1024 <mss 1460>
SENT (0.2804s) TCP 10.10.4.25:60354 > 10.10.4.1:110 S ttl=59 id=19854
iplen=44  seq=1617903748 win=1024 <mss 1460>
SENT (0.2804s) TCP 10.10.4.25:60354 > 10.10.4.1:8080 S ttl=46
id=54919 iplen=44  seq=1617903748 win=1024 <mss 1460>
SENT (0.2805s) TCP 10.10.4.25:60354 > 10.10.4.1:3306 S ttl=41
id=26585 iplen=44  seq=1617903748 win=1024 <mss 1460>
SENT (0.2806s) TCP 10.10.4.25:60354 > 10.10.4.1:5900 S ttl=51
id=13633 iplen=44  seq=1617903748 win=1024 <mss 1460>
SENT (0.2807s) TCP 10.10.4.25:60354 > 10.10.4.1:256 S ttl=48 id=39170
iplen=44  seq=1617903748 win=1024 <mss 1460>
SENT (0.2808s) TCP 10.10.4.25:60354 > 10.10.4.1:23 S ttl=56 id=60892
iplen=44  seq=1617903748 win=1024 <mss 1460>
SENT (0.2808s) TCP 10.10.4.25:60354 > 10.10.4.1:111 S ttl=49 id=55716
iplen=44  seq=1617903748 win=1024 <mss 1460>
SENT (0.2809s) TCP 10.10.4.25:60354 > 10.10.4.1:22 S ttl=57 id=21878
iplen=44  seq=1617903748 win=1024 <mss 1460>
SENT (0.2810s) TCP 10.10.4.25:60354 > 10.10.4.1:1025 S ttl=40
id=27546 iplen=44  seq=1617903748 win=1024 <mss 1460>
RCVD (0.2804s) TCP 10.10.4.1:554 > 10.10.4.25:60354 RA ttl=64 id=4236
iplen=40  seq=0 win=0
[...]
```

Packet trace output

The --packet-trace parameter is another useful tool for troubleshooting. It can be used to check for connectivity issues or determine if Nmap is even able to send packets on your system. The example above shows the typical output of a packet trace which displays detailed information about every packet sent/received to and from the target system.

Tip: *Trace information will rapidly scroll across the screen. Use the more command to see one page at a time. Alternatively, redirect output using nmap --packet-trace 10.10.4.1 > trace.txt to save the trace output to a file called trace.txt.*

Display Host Networking Configuration

The --iflist option displays the network interfaces and routes configured on the local system.

Usage syntax: nmap --iflist

```
$ nmap --iflist

Starting Nmap 6.47 ( http://nmap.org ) at 2015-01-17 11:58 CST
************************INTERFACES************************
DEV     (SHORT)  IP/MASK         TYPE      UP    MTU    MAC
lo      (lo)     127.0.0.1/8     loopback  up    65536
eth0    (eth0)   (null)/0        ethernet  down  1500   00:E0:53:14:51:BB
eth1    (eth1)   (null)/0        ethernet  down  1500   00:1C:C4:8F:80:AC
eth2    (eth2)   10.10.4.1/24    ethernet  up    1500   00:13:3B:10:54:0E
eth2.5  (eth2.5) 10.10.5.1/24    ethernet  up    1500   00:13:3B:10:54:0E
eth3    (eth3)   10.10.3.100/24  ethernet  up    1500   00:13:3B:10:54:0F


**************************ROUTES**************************
DST/MASK                DEV     METRIC GATEWAY
10.10.3.0/24            eth3    0
10.10.4.0/24            eth2    0
10.10.5.0/24            eth2.5  0
0.0.0.0/0               eth3    0      10.10.3.1
```

Interface list output

The above example displays the network and routing information for the local system. This option can be helpful for quickly identifying network configuration or troubleshooting connectivity issues.

Tip: *Additional commands that are helpful for troubleshooting networking configuration include ifconfig (Unix/Linux) and ipconfig (Windows). Most Windows and Unix based systems also include the netstat utility that provides additional network information.*

Specify Which Network Interface to Use

The -e option is used to manually specify which network interface Nmap should use.

Usage syntax: nmap -e [interface] [target]

```
# nmap -e eth0 10.10.3.1

Starting Nmap 6.47 ( http://nmap.org ) at 2015-01-17 12:03 CST
Nmap scan report for 10.10.3.1
Host is up (0.20s latency).
Not shown: 997 closed ports
PORT     STATE SERVICE
22/tcp   open  ssh
80/tcp   open  http
443/tcp  open  https

Nmap done: 1 IP address (1 host up) scanned in 3.74 seconds
```

Manually specifying a network interface

Many systems now have multiple network interfaces. Most modern laptops, for example, have both a regular ethernet jack and a wireless card. If you want to ensure Nmap is using your preferred interface you can use -e to specify it on the command line. In this example -e is used to force Nmap to scan via the eth0 interface on the host system.

Section 11: Zenmap

Overview

Zenmap is a graphical frontend for Nmap designed to make light work of Nmap's complex scanning features. The Zenmap GUI is a cross-platform program that can be used on Windows, Mac OS X, and Unix/Linux systems.

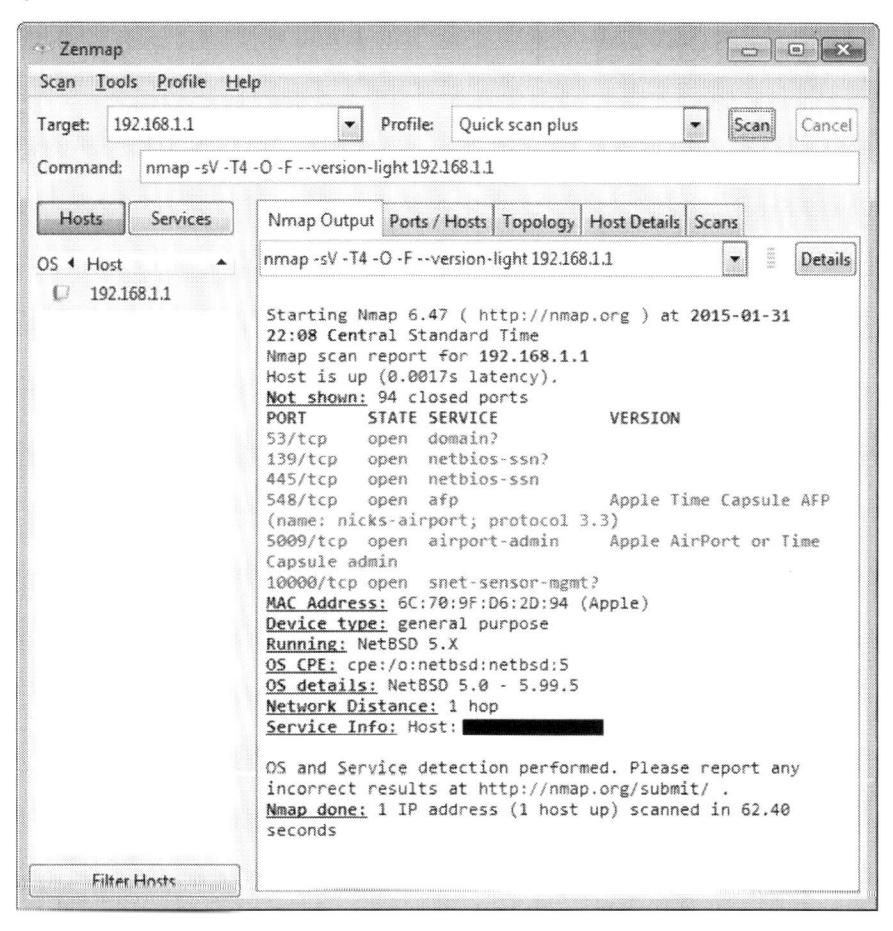

Zenmap GUI

151

Launching Zenmap

Windows Users

Zenmap is installed by default when you install Nmap on Windows systems. To start Zenmap go to Start > Programs > Nmap > Zenmap GUI.

Unix and Linux Users

Zenmap is automatically installed when you compile Nmap from source on a system with a desktop such as Gnome or KDE. If you install Nmap via apt or yum you may have to manually install the Zenmap package. This can be done by executing one of the following commands:

Debian/Ubuntu

```
# apt-get install zenmap
```

Fedora/Red Hat/CentOS

```
# yum install nmap-frontend
```

Once installed, the Zenmap GUI can be launched by locating the icon on your system's application menu.

Mac OS X Users

Zenmap for Mac OS X is installed in Applications > Zenmap. It is included automatically as part of the default Nmap installation.

Note: *The X11 server for Mac OS X is required to run Zenmap on Mac systems. This software can be found on the Mac OS X installation DVD. Newer versions of Mac OS X no longer include X11 server software. The Xquartz program can be installed on these systems in place of the legacy X11 server. Xquartz can be downloaded from xquartz.macosforge.org.*

Basic Zenmap Operations

Performing a scan with Zenmap is as simple as 1, 2, 3...

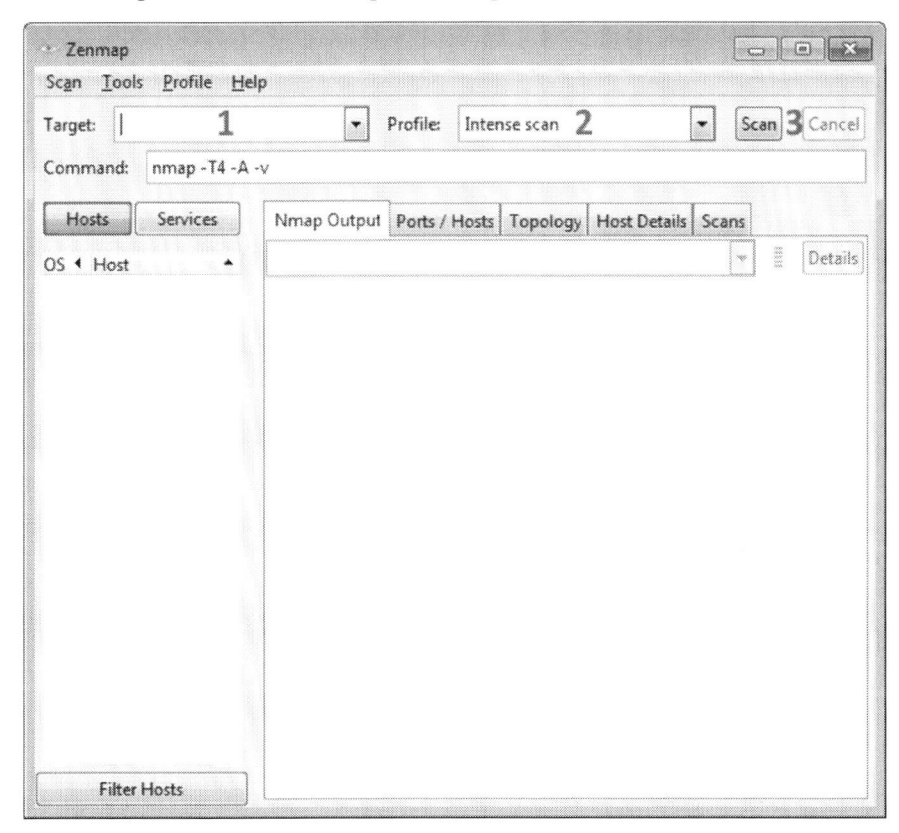

Zenmap GUI overview

Step 1
Enter a target (or select a recent target from the list)

Step 2
Select a scanning profile

Step 3
Press the scan button

153

Zenmap Results

The results of the scan are displayed once the scan is finished. The Nmap Output tab displays the raw output of the scan as it would appear on the command line. Zenmap also keeps a history of your scanning activity. This allows you to reference an earlier scan by selecting it from the sidebar list.

Zenmap scan output

Note: *The actual command line string executed is displayed in the Command box above.*

Scanning Profiles

Zenmap provides built-in profiles for the most common types of scans. This simplifies the scanning process by eliminating the need to manually specify a long string of arguments on the command line.

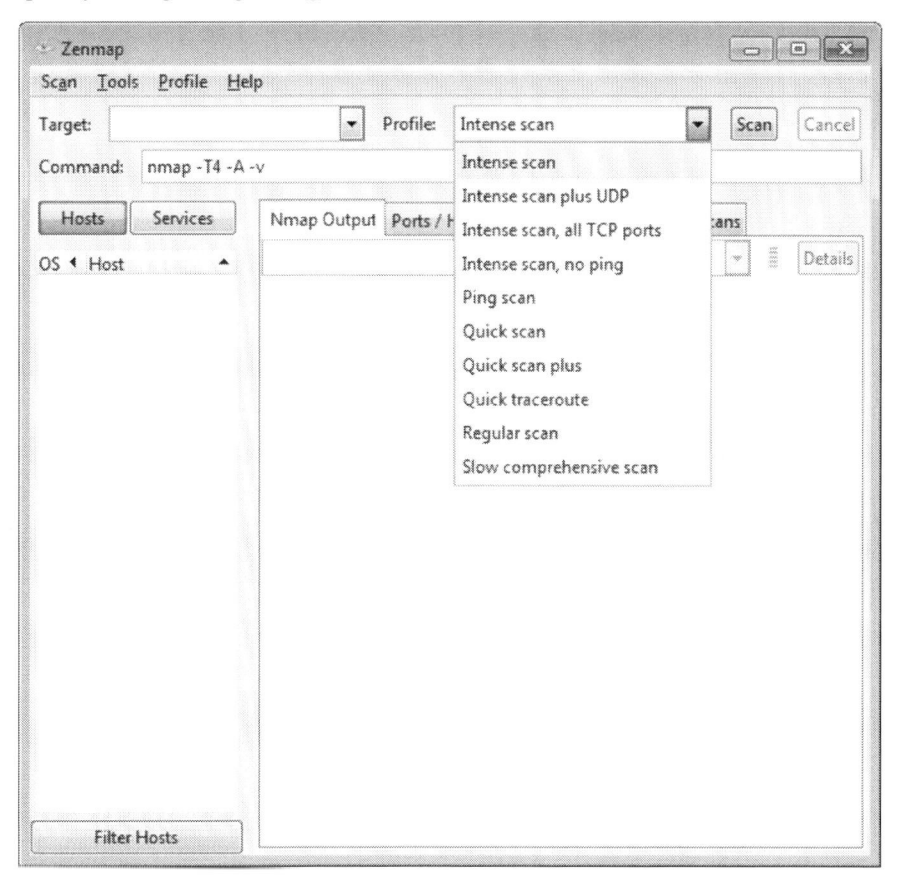

Zenmap scanning profiles

Profile Editor

If the built-in scans don't meet your exact needs, you can create your own scanning profile. To do this, simply access the profile editor by selecting Profile > New Profile from the Zenmap menu (or press <CTRL + P> on the keyboard).

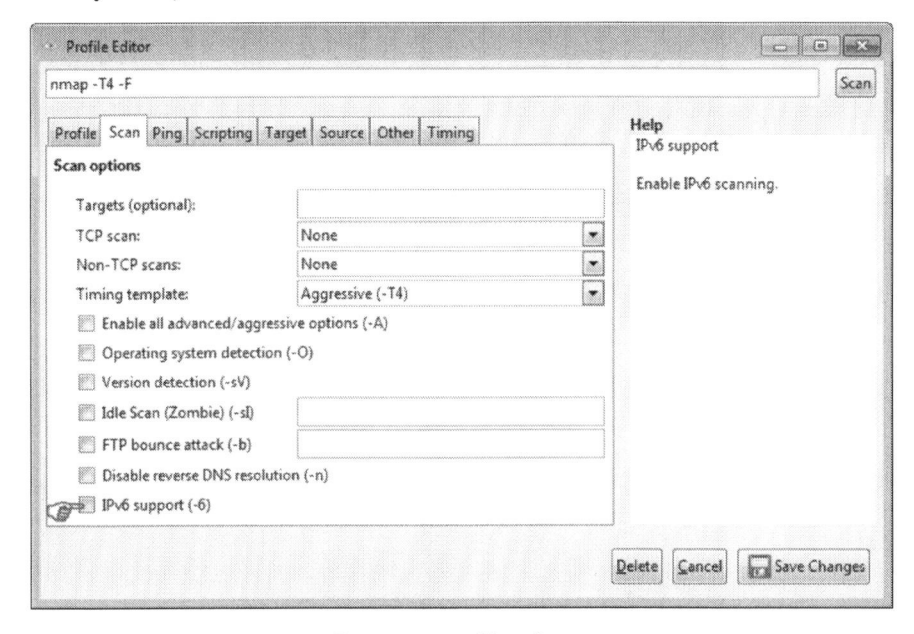

Zenmap profile editor

Within the Zenmap Profile Editor, you can select the options for your custom profile and Zenmap will automatically build the complex Nmap command line string based on your selections.

Tip: *Hovering your mouse over various options will show information about the selection in the help field.*

Once finished, simply click the Save Changes button and your custom profile will be available for use in the profile selection combo-box.

Viewing Open Ports

Once a scan is completed you can view a user-friendly display of the results on the Ports/Hosts tab. The buttons labeled Hosts and Services can be used to toggle the display of the recent scans.

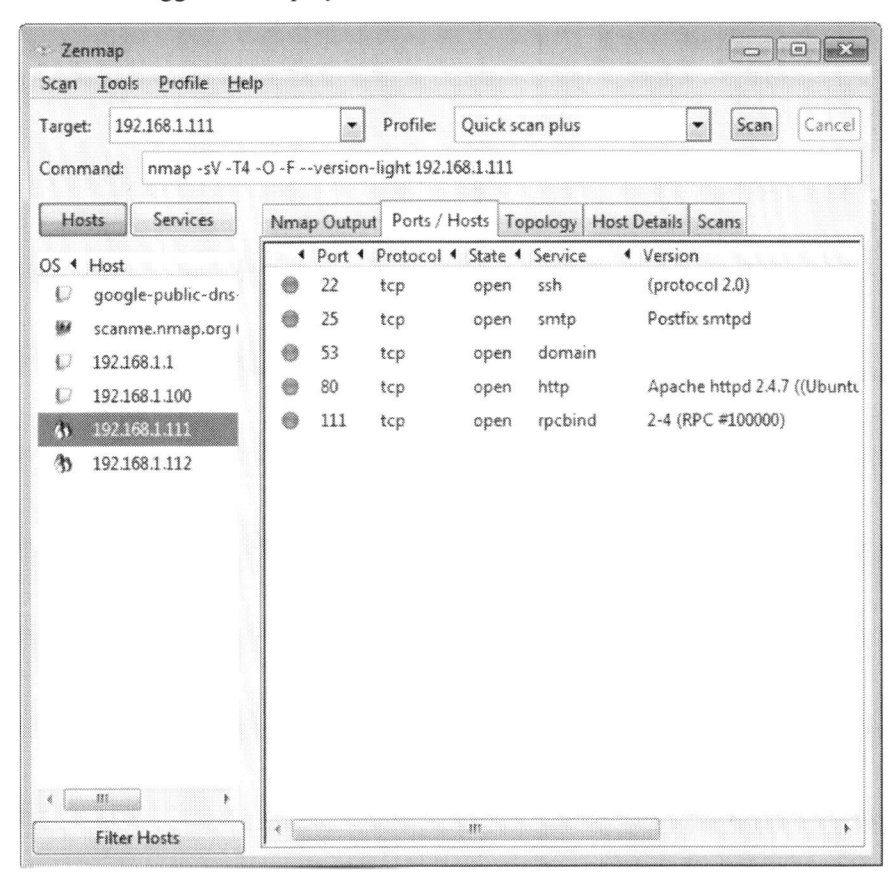

Zenmap ports display

157

Viewing a Network Map

After performing one or more scans, you can view the results on a graphical map on the Topology tab.

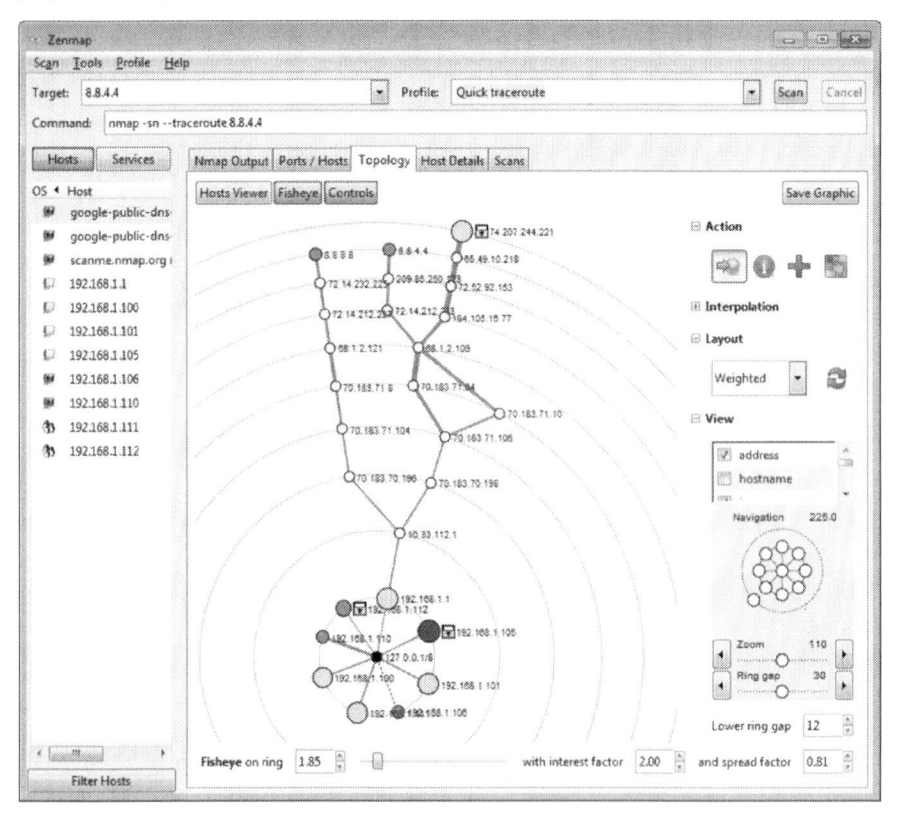

Zenmap topology map

Zenmap's topology feature provides an interactive graphic that shows the layout of a network and path to targets for completed scans (assuming a traceroute enabled profile is selected).

Tip: *The graphic can be manipulated by pressing the Controls button to modify the various display options.*

Saving Network Maps

You can also save a Zenmap topology map by pressing the Save Graphic button.

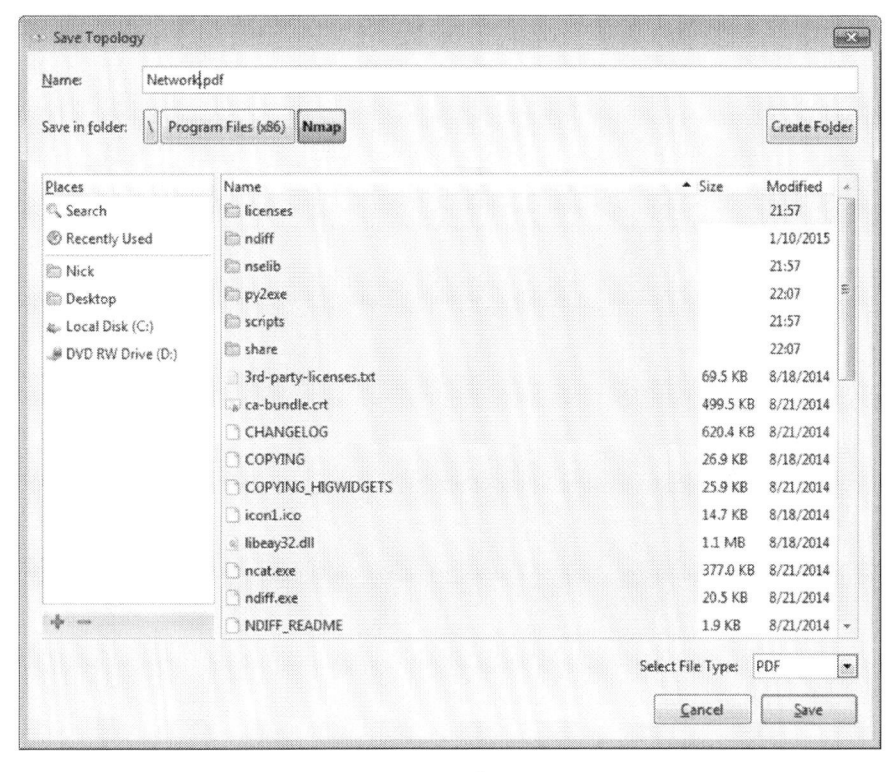

Saving a topology map

Zenmap supports exporting maps to several popular formats including PNG, PDF, SVG, and Postscript.

159

Viewing Host Details

The Host Details tab provides a user-friendly display of information gathered from a target system.

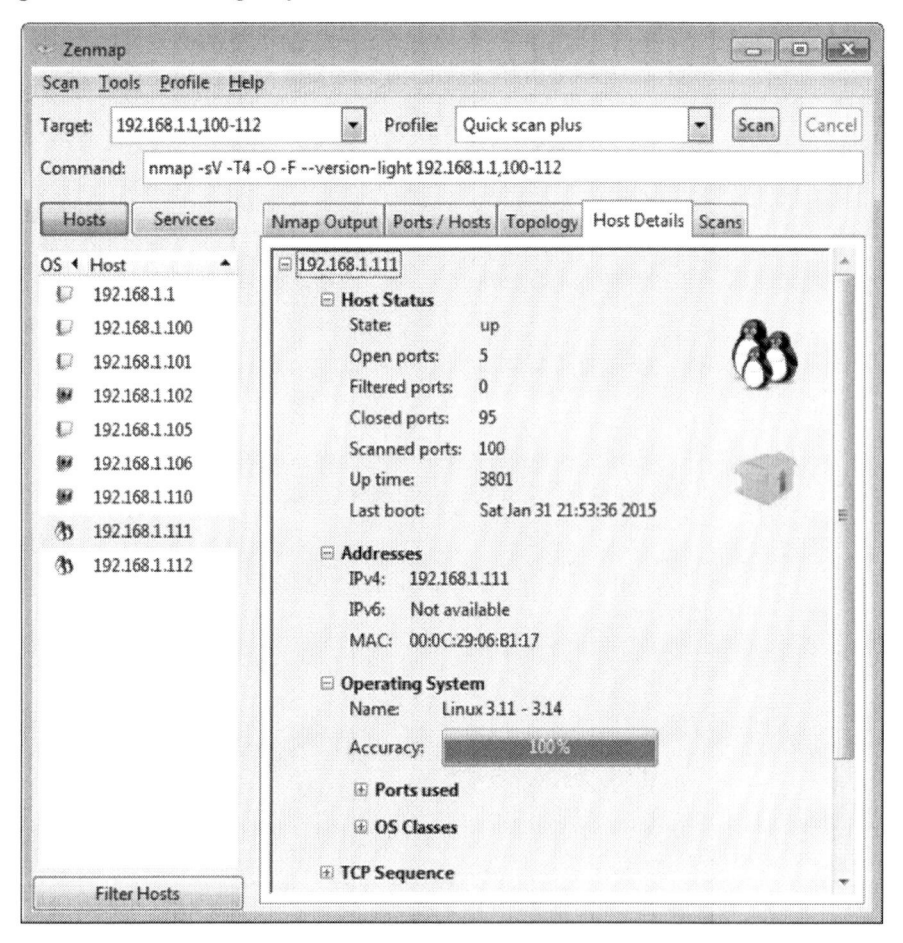

Zenmap host details

Viewing Scan History

The Scans tab displays scanning history for the current session. You can also manage previous scans by using the Add, Remove, or Cancel buttons at the bottom of the screen.

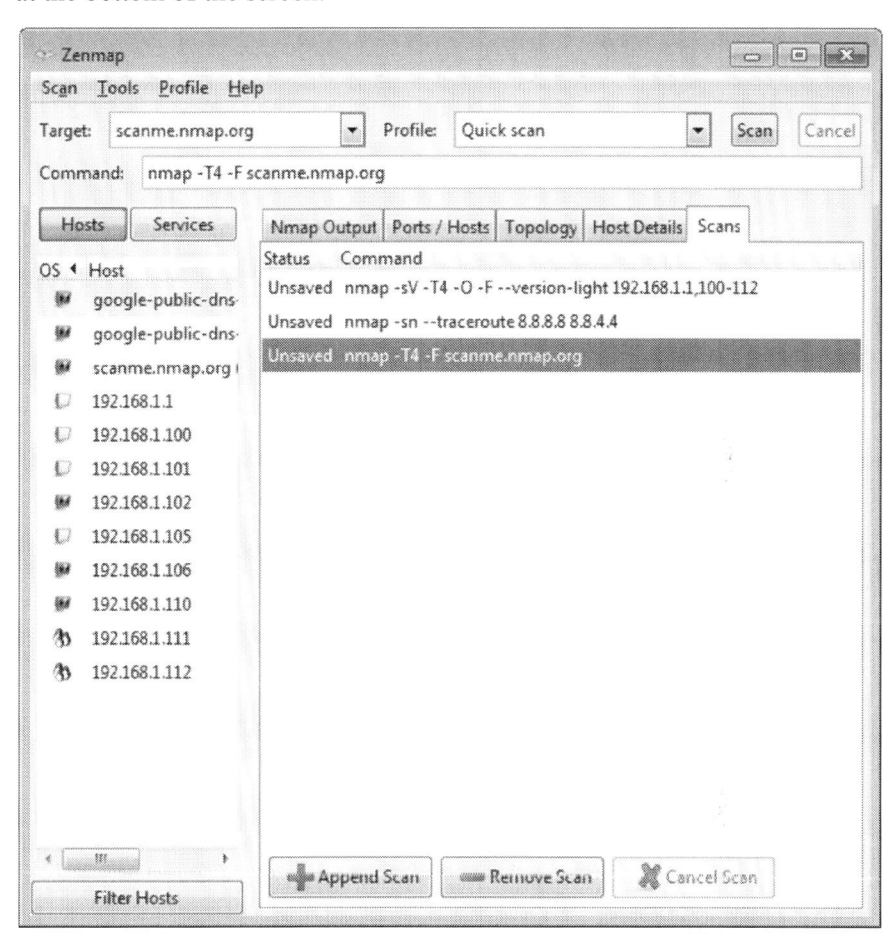

Zenmap scan history

161

Comparing Scan Results

Nmap and Zenmap scans can be compared using the Compare Results feature. To do this, select Tools > Compare Results from the Zenmap menu or press <CTRL + D>.

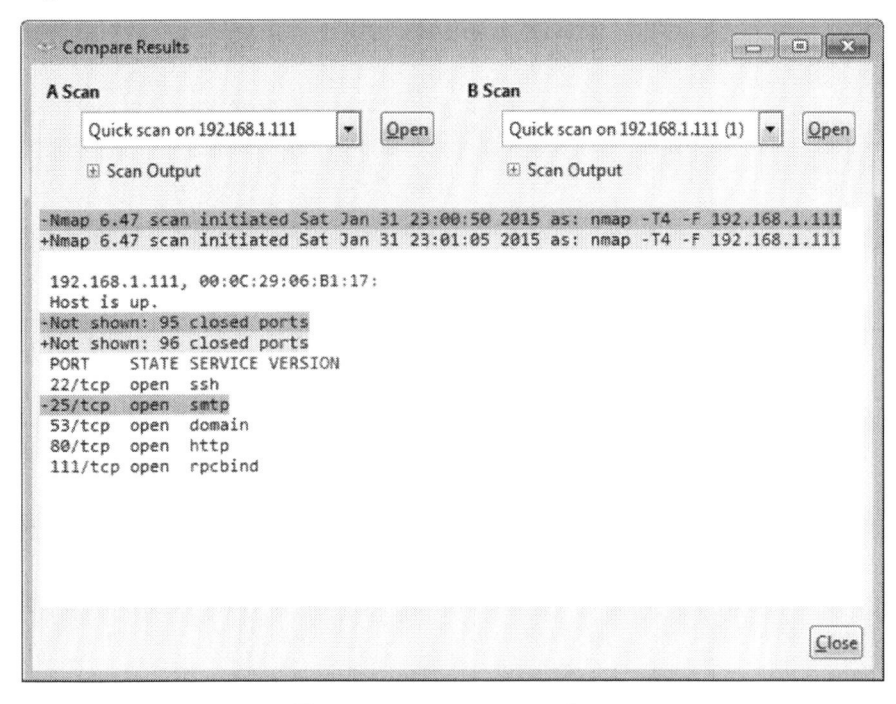

Zenmap comparison utility

Zenmap will load recent scans into the comparison utility or you can import an Nmap XML output file by pressing the Open button. The differences between the two selected scans are highlighted and color-coded for easy comparison.

Saving Scans

Zenmap scans can be saved for future reference by selecting Scan > Save Scan from the menu or pressing <CTRL + S>.

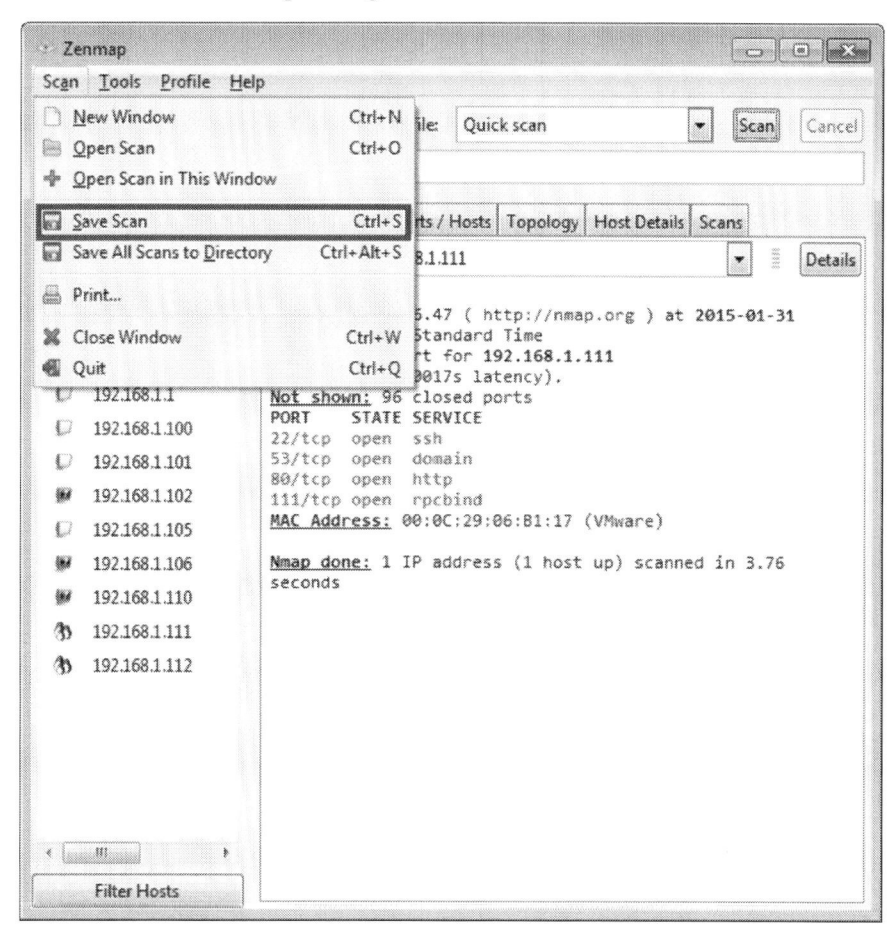

Saving Zenmap scans

163

Section 12: Nmap Scripting Engine (NSE)

Overview

The Nmap Scripting Engine is a powerful tool that allows users to develop custom scripts that can take advantage of Nmap's advanced scanning functions. These scripts can provide additional information about a target system outside of a typical port scan.

In addition to the ability to write your own custom scripts, there are hundreds of standard built-in scripts that offer some interesting features such as vulnerability detection and exploitation. A complete list of the available NSE scripts can be found online at nmap.org/nsedoc/.

Note: *Scripts for NSE are written in the Lua programming language. Unfortunately, programming in Lua is outside the scope of this book. This chapter provides an overview for utilizing the built in scripts. For more information about Lua visit lua.org.*

Warning: *The NSE uses aggressive scanning techniques that can (in some rare cases) cause undesirable results like system downtime and data loss. Additionally, NSE vulnerability exploitation features could get you into legal trouble if you don't have permission to scan the target systems.*

Summary of features covered in this section:

--script [script]
Execute Individual Scripts

--script [script1,script2,etc]
Execute Multiple Scripts

--script [category]
Execute Scripts by Category

script [category1, category2]
Execute Multiple Script Categories

--script-help
Show information about a NSE script

--script-trace
Troubleshoot Scripts

--script-updatedb
Update the Script Database

Execute Individual Scripts

The --script argument is used to execute NSE scripts.

Usage syntax: nmap --script [script.nse] [target]

```
# nmap --script whois-ip.nse scanme.nmap.org

Starting Nmap 6.47 ( http://nmap.org ) at 2015-01-17 12:38 CST
Nmap scan report for scanme.nmap.org (74.207.244.221)
Host is up (0.31s latency).
Not shown: 997 closed ports
PORT      STATE SERVICE
22/tcp    open  ssh
80/tcp    open  http
9929/tcp  open  nping-echo

Host script results:
| whois: Record found at whois.arin.net
| netrange: 74.207.224.0 - 74.207.255.255
| netname: LINODE-US
| orgname: Linode
| orgid: LINOD
| country: US stateprov: NJ
|
| orgtechname: Linode Network Operations
|_orgtechemail: support@***.com

Nmap done: 1 IP address (1 host up) scanned in 4.00 seconds
```

Executing an NSE script

Script results are displayed under the heading "Host script results". In the example above, the --script option is used to execute a script called whois-ip.nse. The built-in whois-ip.nse script retrieves information about the public IP address of the specified target from ARIN (American Registry for Internet Numbers).

This is just one of the numerous built-in NSE scripts. Each new Nmap release brings additional scripts and refinements to existing scripts. A complete list of the built-in scripts for Nmap can be found online at nmap.org/nsedoc/.

Note: *This NSE script was apparently renamed at some point. Version 6.47 uses whois-ip.nse and older versions of Nmap use whois.nse. Try whois.nse if you receive an error using an older version of Nmap.*

Common Scripts

At the time of this writing, there were over 300 NSE scripts listed online at nmap.org/nsedoc/. While all of these scripts are useful, some are more useful than others. The list below describes some of the most useful NSE scripts applicable to everyday situations. You can use this as a starter guide to become familiar with the NSE.

dhcp-discover.nse - Discover information about a DHCP server.

dns-nsid.nse - Display information about a DNS server.

ftp-anon.nse - Check if an FTP server allows anonymous access.

http-errors.nse - Craw a website and list any errors.

http-google-malware.nse - Checks if a given website is on Google's malware blacklist.

http-headers.nse - List the HTTP headers for a webserver.

mysql-info.nse - Display information about MySQL servers.

nbstat.nse - Display NETBIOS information for Windows/Samba systems.

ntp-info.nse - Display information about an NTP server.

smb-os-discovery.nse - Display information about an SMB host.

smtp-commands.nse - Gather information on an SMTP server.

snmp-info.nse - Display information about a system running SNMP.

smtp-open-relay.nse - Test if a server is an open SMTP relay.

whois-ip.nse - Perform a whois lookup on a given IP address.

Tip: *To simplify script selection, the NSE allows for executing scripts using wildcards and grouped categories. These tricks are immensely helpful for executing multiple scripts and are discussed next.*

Execute Multiple Scripts

The Nmap Scripting Engine supports the ability to run multiple scripts concurrently.

Usage syntax: nmap --script [script1,script2,etc|"expression"] [target]

```
$ nmap --script "smtp*" 10.10.4.25

Starting Nmap 6.47 ( http://nmap.org ) at 2015-01-17 12:40 CST
Nmap scan report for 10.10.4.25
Host is up (0.00039s latency).
Not shown: 998 closed ports
PORT    STATE SERVICE
22/tcp  open  ssh
25/tcp  open  smtp
| smtp-brute:
|_  ERROR: Failed to retrieve authentication mechanisms form server
|_smtp-commands: smtp.***.com, PIPELINING, SIZE 20971520, VRFY, ETRN,
STARTTLS, ENHANCEDSTATUSCODES, 8BITMIME, DSN,
| smtp-enum-users:
|   root
|   admin
|   administrator
|   webadmin
|   sysadmin
|   netadmin
|   guest
|   user
|   web
|_  test
|_smtp-open-relay: Server is an open relay (16/16 tests)
| smtp-vuln-cve2010-4344:
|_  The SMTP server is not Exim: NOT VULNERABLE

Nmap done: 1 IP address (1 host up) scanned in 5.23 seconds
```

Executing all SMTP scripts

In this example, the asterisks wildcard character is used to execute all scripts that begin with "smtp". You can also provide a comma-separated list of individual scripts to run using the following syntax: nmap --script script1,script2,etc.

Note: *When using wildcards some systems may require the expression to be enclosed in quotes such as "smtp*" or "ftp*".*

Tip: *Some NSE scripts accept arguments using the --script-args option. This allows you to specify specific parameters for a script. A complete list of arguments for each script can be found online at nmap.org/nsedoc/.*

Execute Scripts by Category

The --script option can also be used to execute multiple scripts based on their category.

Usage syntax: nmap --script [category] [target]

```
# nmap --script default 10.10.4.46

Starting Nmap 6.47 ( http://nmap.org ) at 2015-01-17 12:43 CST
Nmap scan report for 10.10.4.46
Host is up (0.00018s latency).
Not shown: 978 closed ports
PORT      STATE SERVICE
53/tcp    open  domain
| dns-nsid:
|_  bind.version: Microsoft DNS 6.1.7601 (1DB1565C)
[...]
Host script results:
|_nbstat: NetBIOS name: FS1, NetBIOS user: <unknown>, NetBIOS MAC: 00:0c:29:14:9b:ea (VMware)
| smb-os-discovery:
|   OS: Windows Server 2008 R2 Standard 7601 Service Pack 1 (Windows Server 2008 R2 Standard 6.1)
|   OS CPE: cpe:/o:microsoft:windows_server_2008::sp1
|   Computer name: fs1
|   NetBIOS computer name: FS1
|   Domain name: asdf.local
|   Forest name: asdf.local
|   FQDN: fs1.asdf.local
|   NetBIOS domain name: ASDF
|_  System time: 2015-01-17T12:44:15-06:00
| smb-security-mode:
|   Account that was used for smb scripts: guest
|   User-level authentication
|   SMB Security: Challenge/response passwords supported
|_  Message signing required
|_smbv2-enabled: Server supports SMBv2 protocol

Nmap done: 1 IP address (1 host up) scanned in 7.53 seconds
```

Executing all scripts in the default category

Note: *A complete list of categories is provided on the next page.*

By specifying a category with the --script option, Nmap will execute every script in the specified category. In the example above, the results of the scripts in the default category are displayed under the "Host script results" heading. Additional scripts related to open ports are shown directly under their scan results, such as DNS in the above example.

Tip: *The -sC option is a shortcut for --script default that will execute all of the NSE scripts in the default category.*

Script Categories

The NSE --script option supports executing multiple scripts based on category. Each category is a group of related scripts that simplifies script selection. The list below describes the available NSE categories:

all
Runs all available NSE scripts

auth
Scripts related to authentication

default
Runs a basic set of default scripts

discovery
Attempts to discover in depth information about a target

external
Scripts that contact external sources (such as the whois database)

intrusive
Scripts which may be considered intrusive by the target system

malware
Scripts that check for open backdoors and malware

safe
Basic scripts that are not intrusive

vuln
Checks target for commonly exploited vulnerabilities

Using script categories is the easiest way to launch NSE built-in scripts – unless you know the specific script you want to run. Executing scripts by category, however, can take longer to complete since each category contains numerous scripts.

Tip: A complete list of the NSE scripts in each category can be found online at *nmap.org/nsedoc/*.

Execute Multiple Script Categories

Multiple script categories can be executed concurrently using one of the following syntax:

`nmap --script category1,category2,etc`

Specifying multiple script categories as a comma-separated list will execute all scripts in the defined categories. For example, executing nmap --script malware,vuln would run all scripts in the malware and vulnerabilities categories.

`nmap --script "category1 and category2"`

NSE scripts can belong to more than one category. The "and" operator can be used to take advantage of this by executing all scripts that belong to both of the specified categories. For example, nmap --script "default and safe" would only execute scripts that belong to both the default and safe categories.

`nmap --script "category1 or category2"`

The "or" operator can be used to run scripts that belong to either of the specified categories. For example, nmap --script "default or safe" would execute all scripts that belong to either the default or safe categories.

`nmap --script "not category"`

The "not" operator is used to exclude scripts that belong to the specified category. For example, executing nmap --script "not intrusive" would run all scripts that do not belong to the intrusive category.

Show Script Help Files

The --script-help option can be used to display helpful information about a script.

Usage syntax: nmap --script-help [script]

```
# nmap --script-help whois-ip.nse

Starting Nmap 6.47 ( http://nmap.org ) at 2015-01-27 04:16 CST

whois-ip
Categories: discovery external safe
http://nmap.org/nsedoc/scripts/whois-ip.html
Queries the WHOIS services of Regional Internet Registries (RIR) and
attempts to retrieve information about the IP Address Assignment
which contains the Target IP Address.
[...]
```

Displaying NSE script help

In this example, the --script-help option is used to show a summary of helpful information about the whois-ip.nse script's purpose. This can be handy in situations where you don't have internet access to read the official NSE documentation online.

Tip: *You can also read the help summary for scripts by specifying a category as the argument to --script-help. For example, executing "***nmap --script-help default | more***" would show the help information for all files in the default category.*

Troubleshoot Scripts

The --script-trace option is used to trace NSE scripts.

Usage syntax: nmap --script [script(s)] --script-trace [target]

```
# nmap --script default --script-trace 10.10.4.1 | more
4.1:22] (timeout: 30000ms) EID 282
NSOCK INFO [1.9310s] nsock_trace_handler_callback(): Callback: READ
SUCCESS for EID 282 [10.10.4.1:22] (1648 bytes)
NSOCK INFO [1.9310s] nsi_new2(): nsi_new (IOD #7)
NSOCK INFO [1.9310s] nsock_connect_tcp(): TCP connection requested to
[...]
NSE: TCP 10.10.4.25:48682 > 10.10.4.1:22 | CLOSE
NSE: TCP 10.10.4.25:48683 > 10.10.4.1:22 | CONNECT
NSE: TCP 10.10.4.25:48683 < 10.10.4.1:22 | SSH-2.0-OpenSSH_6.6.1p1
Ubuntu-2ubuntu2
[...]
```

NSE trace output

The --script-trace option displays all information sent and received by the NSE and is useful for troubleshooting problems related to scripts.

Some scripts can generate hundreds of lines of output when using the script trace option. In most cases, it is better to redirect the output to a file for later review. The example below demonstrates how to do this.

```
# nmap --script default 10.10.4.1 --script-trace > trace.txt
```

Redirecting the output of an NSE trace

The resulting trace.txt file will contain all of the trace data and can be viewed in a standard text editor.

173

Update the Script Database

The --script-updatedb option is used to update the script database.

Usage syntax: nmap --script-updatedb

```
# nmap --script-updatedb

Starting Nmap 6.47 ( http://nmap.org ) at 2015-01-17 12:50 CST
NSE: Updating rule database.
NSE: Script Database updated successfully.
Nmap done: 0 IP addresses (0 hosts up) scanned in 0.99 seconds
```

Updating the NSE script database

Nmap maintains a database of scripts that is used to facilitate the option of executing multiple scripts via category. Most Unix-like systems store scripts in the /usr/share/nmap/scripts/ directory. Windows systems store these files in C:\Program Files\Nmap\scripts. If you add or remove scripts from the scripts directory you must run nmap --script-updatedb to apply the changes to the script database.

Section 13: Ndiff

Overview

Ndiff is a tool within the Nmap suite that allows you to compare two scans and flag any changes between them. It accepts two Nmap XML output files and highlights the differences between each file for easy comparison. Ndiff can be used on the command line or in GUI form within the Zenmap application.

Summary of features covered in this section:

ndiff
Comparison Using Ndiff

-v
Ndiff Verbose Mode

--xml
XML Output Mode

Scan Comparison Using Ndiff

The ndiff utility is used to perform a comparison of two Nmap scans.

Usage syntax: ndiff [file1.xml file2.xml]

```
$ ndiff scan1.xml scan2.xml
-Nmap 6.47 scan initiated Sat Jan 17 12:52:38 2015 as: nmap -oX
scan1.xml 10.10.4.25
+Nmap 6.47 scan initiated Sat Jan 17 12:52:53 2015 as: nmap -oX
scan2.xml 10.10.4.25

 10.10.4.25:
-Not shown: 998 closed ports
+Not shown: 999 closed ports
 PORT   STATE SERVICE VERSION
-25/tcp open  smtp
```

Comparison of two Nmap scans

Basic usage of the Ndiff utility consists of comparing two Nmap XML output files. Differences between the two files are highlighted with a minus sign indicating the information in the first file and the plus sign indicating the changes within the second file. In the above example we see that port 25 on the second scan has changed states when compared to the first scan.

Ndiff Verbose Mode

The -v option is used to display verbose output with Ndiff.

Usage syntax: ndiff -v [file1.xml file2.xml]

```
$ ndiff -v scan1.xml scan2.xml
-Nmap 6.47 scan initiated Sat Jan 17 12:52:38 2015 as: nmap -oX
scan1.xml 10.10.4.25
+Nmap 6.47 scan initiated Sat Jan 17 12:52:53 2015 as: nmap -oX
scan2.xml 10.10.4.25

 10.10.4.25:
 Host is up.
-Not shown: 998 closed ports
+Not shown: 999 closed ports
 PORT    STATE SERVICE VERSION
 22/tcp open   ssh
-25/tcp open   smtp
```

Output of a Ndiff scan in verbose mode

The verbose output displays all lines of both XML files and highlights the differences with a minus sign indicating the information in the first file and the plus sign indicating the changes within the second file. This is in contrast to the default ndiff behavior which only displays the differences between the two files. Verbose output is often more helpful than the default output, as it displays all information regardless whether or not there are differences.

XML Output Mode

The -xml option is used to generate XML output with Ndiff.

Usage syntax: ndiff --xml [file1.xml] [file2.xml]

```
$ ndiff --xml scan1.xml scan2.xml | more
<?xml version="1.0" encoding="utf-8"?>
<nmapdiff version="1"><scandiff><a><nmaprun args="nmap -oX scan1.xml
10.10.4.25" scanner="nmap" start="1421520758" startstr="Sat Jan 17
12:52:38 2015" version="6.47"/>
</a><b><nmaprun args="nmap -oX scan2.xml 10.10.4.25" scanner="nmap"
start="1421520773" startstr="Sat Jan 17 12:52:53 2015"
version="6.47"/>
</b><hostdiff>
<host>
<address addr="10.10.4.25" addrtype="ipv4"/>
<ports>
<a>
<extraports count="998" state="closed"/>
</a>
<b>
<extraports count="999" state="closed"/>
</b>
<portdiff>
<a>
<port portid="25" protocol="tcp">
<state state="open"/>
<service name="smtp"/>
</port>
</a>
[...]
```

Ndiff XML output

XML output is a great tool for feeding information from Ndiff into a third party program using a widely supported format.

Tip: *The default --xml output displays the XML code on the screen. To save this information file, type ndiff --xml scan1.xml scan2.xml >ndiff.xml which will redirect the output to a file called ndiff.xml.*

Section 14: Nping

Overview

Nping is a new addition to the Nmap suite. It is thought of as a modern replacement to the traditional ping program shipped on most operating systems. Nping is also considered a modern replacement for the Hping utility. Hping was a popular ping alternative until it ceased development in 2005. The Nmap project has picked up where Hping left off by providing similar functionality while adding even more powerful features. Nping is "ping on steroids".

Summary of features covered in this section:

-H
Hide sent packets

-q
Hide all packets

-c
Specify a ping count

--rate
Specify a ping rate

--delay
Specify a ping delay

--data-length
Generate a payload

--tcp
Ping using TCP

--udp
Ping using UDP

-p
Ping a specific port

--arp
Perform an ARP ping

Perform a Simple Ping

Executing Nping with no options will send 5 ICMP pings to the specified target.

Usage syntax: nping [target]

```
# nping 192.168.1.1

Starting Nping 0.6.47 ( http://nmap.org/nping ) at 2015-01-23 18:19 CST
SENT (0.0039s) ICMP [192.168.1.100 > 192.168.1.1 Echo request (type=8/code=0) id=8877 seq=1] IP [ttl=64 id=45140 iplen=28 ]
RCVD (0.0069s) ICMP [192.168.1.1 > 192.168.1.100 Echo reply (type=0/code=0) id=8877 seq=1] IP [ttl=255 id=0 iplen=28 ]
SENT (1.0079s) ICMP [192.168.1.100 > 192.168.1.1 Echo request (type=8/code=0) id=8877 seq=2] IP [ttl=64 id=45140 iplen=28 ]
RCVD (1.0110s) ICMP [192.168.1.1 > 192.168.1.100 Echo reply (type=0/code=0) id=8877 seq=2] IP [ttl=255 id=0 iplen=28 ]
SENT (2.0105s) ICMP [192.168.1.100 > 192.168.1.1 Echo request (type=8/code=0) id=8877 seq=3] IP [ttl=64 id=45140 iplen=28 ]
RCVD (2.0134s) ICMP [192.168.1.1 > 192.168.1.100 Echo reply (type=0/code=0) id=8877 seq=3] IP [ttl=255 id=0 iplen=28 ]
SENT (3.0165s) ICMP [192.168.1.100 > 192.168.1.1 Echo request (type=8/code=0) id=8877 seq=4] IP [ttl=64 id=45140 iplen=28 ]
RCVD (3.0195s) ICMP [192.168.1.1 > 192.168.1.100 Echo reply (type=0/code=0) id=8877 seq=4] IP [ttl=255 id=0 iplen=28 ]
SENT (4.0204s) ICMP [192.168.1.100 > 192.168.1.1 Echo request (type=8/code=0) id=8877 seq=5] IP [ttl=64 id=45140 iplen=28 ]
RCVD (4.0234s) ICMP [192.168.1.1 > 192.168.1.100 Echo reply (type=0/code=0) id=8877 seq=5] IP [ttl=255 id=0 iplen=28 ]

Max rtt: 2.870ms | Min rtt: 2.704ms | Avg rtt: 2.775ms
Raw packets sent: 5 (140B) | Rcvd: 5 (140B) | Lost: 0 (0.00%)
Nping done: 1 IP address pinged in 4.02 seconds
```

Pinging a system with Nping

By default, Nping sends 5 ping packets and then quits. A summary is then displayed at the end of the session. Nping differs from traditional ping programs by showing ping packets sent in both directions. Packets marked SENT are for outgoing pings and packets marked RCVD represent the reply. The nping command also displays helpful information contained in the packet headers such as the TTL and packet length.

Tip: *Nping works best when it runs with root privileges on Unix/Linux/Mac. This is the default mode of operation on Windows systems.*

Hide Sent Packets

The -H option can be used to hide sent ping packets.

Usage syntax: nping -H [target]

```
# nping -H 192.168.1.1
```

```
Starting Nping 0.6.47 ( http://nmap.org/nping ) at 2015-01-23 18:23 CST
RCVD (0.0070s) ICMP [192.168.1.1 > 192.168.1.100 Echo reply
(type=0/code=0) id=61279 seq=1] IP [ttl=255 id=0 iplen=28 ]
RCVD (1.0078s) ICMP [192.168.1.1 > 192.168.1.100 Echo reply
(type=0/code=0) id=61279 seq=2] IP [ttl=255 id=0 iplen=28 ]
RCVD (2.0117s) ICMP [192.168.1.1 > 192.168.1.100 Echo reply
(type=0/code=0) id=61279 seq=3] IP [ttl=255 id=0 iplen=28 ]
RCVD (3.0111s) ICMP [192.168.1.1 > 192.168.1.100 Echo reply
(type=0/code=0) id=61279 seq=4] IP [ttl=255 id=0 iplen=28 ]
RCVD (4.0148s) ICMP [192.168.1.1 > 192.168.1.100 Echo reply
(type=0/code=0) id=61279 seq=5] IP [ttl=255 id=0 iplen=28 ]

Max rtt: 2.883ms | Min rtt: 0.973ms | Avg rtt: 2.162ms
Raw packets sent: 5 (140B) | Rcvd: 5 (140B) | Lost: 0 (0.00%)
Nping done: 1 IP address pinged in 4.02 seconds
```

Hiding sent packets

Unlike traditional ping programs that only print replies and errors, Nping prints both sent and received packets. The -H option can be used to hide the sent ping packets. This simulates the traditional ping output behavior and makes the output easier to read when examining responses. The -H option is also helpful when pinging multiple hosts (covered later in this chapter).

Note: *To improve readability the -H option will be used on many of the examples in the remainder of this chapter.*

Hide All Packets

The -q option hides all sent and received ping packets.

Usage syntax: nping -q [target]

```
# nping -q 192.168.1.1

Starting Nping 0.6.47 ( http://nmap.org/nping ) at 2015-01-23 18:31 CST
Max rtt: 3.236ms | Min rtt: 2.586ms | Avg rtt: 2.829ms
Raw packets sent: 5 (140B) | Rcvd: 5 (140B) | Lost: 0 (0.00%)
Nping done: 1 IP address pinged in 4.02 second
```

Hiding all packet output with Nping

The -q option (short for quiet) hides the packet display completely. A summary is still displayed at the end of the session. This option is helpful when doing network stress testing, which is covered later in this chapter. Using the -q option in stress tests helps prevent seizure-inducing output from taking over your display as hundreds of packets per a second volley back and forth.

Specify A Ping Count

The -c option allows you to specify the number of ping packets to send.

Usage syntax: nping -c [count] [target]

```
# nping -H -c 50 192.168.1.1

Starting Nping 0.6.47 ( http://nmap.org/nping ) at 2015-01-23 18:39 CST

RCVD (0.0070s) ICMP [192.168.1.1 > 192.168.1.100 Echo reply
(type=0/code=0) id=50587 seq=1] IP [ttl=255 id=0 iplen=28 ]

[...]

RCVD (49.1901s) ICMP [192.168.1.1 > 192.168.1.100 Echo reply
(type=0/code=0) id=50587 seq=50] IP [ttl=255 id=0 iplen=28 ]

Max rtt: 2.927ms | Min rtt: 1.095ms | Avg rtt: 2.748ms
Raw packets sent: 50 (1.400KB) | Rcvd: 50 (1.400KB) | Lost: 0 (0.00%)
Nping done: 1 IP address pinged in 49.19 seconds
```

Sending 50 pings

By default, Nping sends 5 pings and then quits. In the above example, the -c option is used to override the default count and send 50 pings to the specified target. You can also use **-c 0** to instruct nping to run continuously until interrupted (by pressing <CTRL+ C>).

Ping Multiple Targets

The nping program allows you to specify multiple hosts as targets using the same syntax supported by the nmap command.

Usage syntax: nping [target1 target2 etc | range | CIDR]

```
# nping -H -c 2 192.168.1.1 192.168.1.5

Starting Nping 0.6.47 ( http://nmap.org/nping ) at 2015-01-24 09:24 CST
RCVD (0.0122s) ICMP [192.168.1.1 > 192.168.1.100 Echo reply
(type=0/code=0) id=27395 seq=1] IP [ttl=255 id=0 iplen=28 ]
RCVD (1.0166s) ICMP [192.168.1.5 > 192.168.1.100 Echo reply
(type=0/code=0) id=64201 seq=1] IP [ttl=64 id=56187 iplen=28 ]
RCVD (2.0182s) ICMP [192.168.1.1 > 192.168.1.100 Echo reply
(type=0/code=0) id=27395 seq=2] IP [ttl=255 id=0 iplen=28 ]
RCVD (3.0225s) ICMP [192.168.1.5 > 192.168.1.100 Echo reply
(type=0/code=0) id=64201 seq=2] IP [ttl=64 id=56188 iplen=28 ]

Statistics for host 192.168.1.1:
 |  Probes Sent: 2 | Rcvd: 2 | Lost: 0  (0.00%)
 |_ Max rtt: 2.951ms | Min rtt: 2.843ms | Avg rtt: 2.897ms
Statistics for host 192.168.1.5:
 |  Probes Sent: 2 | Rcvd: 2 | Lost: 0  (0.00%)
 |_ Max rtt: 2.949ms | Min rtt: 1.464ms | Avg rtt: 2.206ms
Raw packets sent: 4 (112B) | Rcvd: 4 (148B) | Lost: 0 (0.00%)
Nping done: 2 IP addresses pinged in 3.02 seconds
```

Pinging two hosts at the same time

In the above example, two hosts are specified (separated by a space). Targets can be specified using ranges, CIDR notation, or DNS names. Each host is pinged in round-robin fashion for the specified number of rounds. At the end of the session, a summary for each host is displayed.

Tip: *Since the targets in the above scan are on the same subnet, you could use the shorthand notation of nping 192.168.1.1,5 to achieve the same results.*

Specify a Ping Rate

The --rate option pings hosts at the specified rate.

Usage syntax: nping --rate [rate] [target]

```
# nping -H --rate 5 192.168.1.1

Starting Nping 0.6.47 ( http://nmap.org/nping ) at 2015-01-23 18:36 CST
RCVD (0.0069s) ICMP [192.168.1.1 > 192.168.1.100 Echo reply
(type=0/code=0) id=53451 seq=1] IP [ttl=255 id=0 iplen=28 ]
RCVD (0.2053s) ICMP [192.168.1.1 > 192.168.1.100 Echo reply
(type=0/code=0) id=53451 seq=2] IP [ttl=255 id=0 iplen=28 ]
RCVD (0.4095s) ICMP [192.168.1.1 > 192.168.1.100 Echo reply
(type=0/code=0) id=53451 seq=3] IP [ttl=255 id=0 iplen=28 ]
RCVD (0.6147s) ICMP [192.168.1.1 > 192.168.1.100 Echo reply
(type=0/code=0) id=53451 seq=4] IP [ttl=255 id=0 iplen=28 ]
RCVD (0.8189s) ICMP [192.168.1.1 > 192.168.1.100 Echo reply
(type=0/code=0) id=53451 seq=5] IP [ttl=255 id=0 iplen=28 ]

Max rtt: 2.768ms | Min rtt: 0.916ms | Avg rtt: 1.363ms
Raw packets sent: 5 (140B) | Rcvd: 5 (140B) | Lost: 0 (0.00%)
Nping done: 1 IP address pinged in 0.82 seconds
```

Specifying a ping rate

The --rate option is used to specify the number of pings to be sent per second. By default, nping sends 1 packet per second. In the above example, specifying --rate 5 instructs Nping to send 5 pings per second. This can be useful when you want to flood a network link to test its robustness, as demonstrated in the next example.

```
# nping -q -c 60000 --rate 1000 192.168.1.1

Starting Nping 0.6.47 ( http://nmap.org/nping ) at 2015-01-24 20:57 CST
Max rtt: 2.509ms | Min rtt: 0.017ms | Avg rtt: 0.017ms
Raw packets sent: 60000 (1.680MB) | Rcvd: 59619 (1.669MB) | Lost: 381 (0.64%)
Nping done: 1 IP address pinged in 60.83 seconds
```

Flooding a network connection with packets

In this example, the --rate option is combined with -c 60000 to attempt to send 1,000 packets per second to the specified target for approximately one minute. The -q (quiet) option is useful in this situation. Notice how there was a loss of 381 packets. This indicates the network was unable to handle the full load of packets. You should note that the source of the lost packets can be the target, link, or even the sending host's network interface if it is unable to handle the return load.

Tip: *The -N option can be used to instruct nping to ignore replies. This can help prevent overwhelming the local system's resources when flooding a target, although nping will not be able to display useful information as a result.*

Specify a Ping Delay

The --delay option allows you to specify a delay between ping probes.

Usage syntax: nping --delay [delay] [target]

```
# nping -H --delay 200ms 192.168.1.1

Starting Nping 0.6.47 ( http://nmap.org/nping ) at 2015-01-23 18:50 CST
RCVD (0.0069s) ICMP [192.168.1.1 > 192.168.1.100 Echo reply
(type=0/code=0) id=28008 seq=1] IP [ttl=255 id=0 iplen=28 ]
RCVD (0.2101s) ICMP [192.168.1.1 > 192.168.1.100 Echo reply
(type=0/code=0) id=28008 seq=2] IP [ttl=255 id=0 iplen=28 ]
RCVD (0.4143s) ICMP [192.168.1.1 > 192.168.1.100 Echo reply
(type=0/code=0) id=28008 seq=3] IP [ttl=255 id=0 iplen=28 ]
RCVD (0.6185s) ICMP [192.168.1.1 > 192.168.1.100 Echo reply
(type=0/code=0) id=28008 seq=4] IP [ttl=255 id=0 iplen=28 ]
RCVD (0.8185s) ICMP [192.168.1.1 > 192.168.1.100 Echo reply
(type=0/code=0) id=28008 seq=5] IP [ttl=255 id=0 iplen=28 ]

Max rtt: 2.774ms | Min rtt: 0.898ms | Avg rtt: 1.365ms
Raw packets sent: 5 (140B) | Rcvd: 5 (140B) | Lost: 0 (0.00%)
Nping done: 1 IP address pinged in 0.82 seconds
```

Specifying a 200ms delay

In this example, the --delay 200ms specifies a 200-millisecond delay. You can use any form of time for the --delay parameter such as milliseconds (ms), seconds (s), minutes (m), or hours (h). For example, --delay 2s would send one packet every two seconds and --delay 1m would send one packet every minute. You can also use decimals such as --delay .5m which would send one packet every 30 seconds.

Note: *The default parameter is seconds when no qualifier is specified.*

Generate a Payload

The --data-length option can be used to send random data as a payload.

Usage syntax: nping --data-length [length] [target]

```
# nping -q --rate 1000 -c 60000 --data-length 1400 192.168.1.1

Starting Nping 0.6.47 ( http://nmap.org/nping ) at 2015-01-24 20:53 CST
Max rtt: 9.143ms | Min rtt: 0.017ms | Avg rtt: 0.017ms
Raw packets sent: 60000 (85.680MB) | Rcvd: 60000 (85.680MB) | Lost: 0 (0.00%)
Nping done: 1 IP address pinged in 61.62 seconds
```

Sending a 1400-byte payload at a rate of 1,000 packets a second

The nping command sends empty packets by default. The --data-length option enables you to send a specific amount of data along with the packet. The program will then generate random data to be transmitted with the ping. This can be useful for testing how well a system handles sustained loads of data. In this example, 85MB of traffic is sent to the target in approximately one minute. No packets are lost during the session indicating a healthy connection.

Tip: *You can also send custom data using the --data or --data-string options.*

Ping Using TCP or UDP

The --tcp and --udp options enable you to ping TCP or UDP ports.

Usage syntax: nping --tcp|--udp [target]

```
# nping -H --tcp W.X.Y.Z

Starting Nping 0.6.47 ( http://nmap.org/nping ) at 2015-01-24 21:58
CST
RCVD (0.0609s) TCP W.X.Y.Z:80 > 192.168.1.100:18983 SA ttl=55 id=2845
iplen=44  seq=2822863765 win=29200 <mss 556>
RCVD (1.0683s) TCP W.X.Y.Z:80 > 192.168.1.100:18983 SA ttl=55
id=23228 iplen=44  seq=1085309427 win=29200 <mss 556>
RCVD (2.0799s) TCP W.X.Y.Z:80 > 192.168.1.100:18983 SA ttl=55
id=16472 iplen=44  seq=3240730386 win=29200 <mss 556>
RCVD (3.0767s) TCP W.X.Y.Z:80 > 192.168.1.100:18983 SA ttl=55
id=50696 iplen=44  seq=1908815270 win=29200 <mss 556>
RCVD (4.0750s) TCP W.X.Y.Z:80 > 192.168.1.100:18983 SA ttl=55
id=39640 iplen=44  seq=3512659904 win=29200 <mss 556>

Max rtt: 65.434ms | Min rtt: 49.115ms | Avg rtt: 57.350ms
Raw packets sent: 5 (200B) | Rcvd: 5 (220B) | Lost: 0 (0.00%)
Nping done: 1 IP address pinged in 4.08 seconds
```

Pinging using the TCP protocol.

Note: The public IP address used in this example is changed to W.X.Y.Z for privacy reasons.

The --tcp and --udp options allow you to ping a system using transport protocols rather than ICMP. This is helpful for checking the liveliness of a firewalled system that does not respond to ICMP probes. It can also be helpful for checking internet facing services running behind a NAT firewall, as the probes will reach the internal port-forwarded destination (rather than stopping at the firewall). Good examples of this are SMTP, DNS, and HTTP, which usually reside behind a NAT firewall.

In the above example, the --tcp option is used to ping a system behind a NAT firewall that does not respond to ICMP pings. For comparison, output for a traditional ping of the same system is shown below.

```
# ping -c4 W.X.Y.Z
PING W.X.Y.Z (W.X.Y.Z): 56 data bytes
Request timeout for icmp_seq 0
Request timeout for icmp_seq 1
Request timeout for icmp_seq 2
Request timeout for icmp_seq 3

--- W.X.Y.Z ping statistics ---
4 packets transmitted, 0 packets received, 100.0% packet loss
```

Note: *The default port for --tcp is 80 and 53 for --udp. You can specify a specific port using the -p option (discussed next).*

Ping Specific Ports (TCP or UDP)

The -p option allows you to specify one or more ports to ping.

Usage syntax: nping --tcp|--udp -p [ports] [target]

```
# nping -H --tcp -p 25 192.168.1.103

Starting Nping 0.6.47 ( http://nmap.org/nping ) at 2015-01-25 03:00 CST
RCVD (0.5595s) TCP 192.168.1.103:25 > 192.168.1.100:22424 SA ttl=64 id=0 iplen=44  seq=4241054482 win=29200 <mss 1460>
RCVD (1.0139s) TCP 192.168.1.103:25 > 192.168.1.100:22424 SA ttl=64 id=0 iplen=44  seq=4248155670 win=29200 <mss 1460>
RCVD (2.0175s) TCP 192.168.1.103:25 > 192.168.1.100:22424 SA ttl=64 id=0 iplen=44  seq=4263835629 win=29200 <mss 1460>
RCVD (3.0247s) TCP 192.168.1.103:25 > 192.168.1.100:22424 SA ttl=64 id=0 iplen=44  seq=4279574586 win=29200 <mss 1460>
RCVD (4.0300s) TCP 192.168.1.103:25 > 192.168.1.100:22424 SA ttl=64 id=0 iplen=44  seq=314719 win=29200 <mss 1460>

Max rtt: 554.722ms | Min rtt: 2.345ms | Avg rtt: 113.858ms
Raw packets sent: 5 (200B) | Rcvd: 5 (220B) | Lost: 0 (0.00%)
Nping done: 1 IP address pinged in 4.03 seconds
```

Performing a TCP ping on port 25

The nping command uses port 80 for TCP and port 53 for UDP by default when pinging via transport protocols. The -p option enables you to ping any port(s). You can specify a single port, comma separated list, or range using the same syntax supported by the nmap command. If multiple ports are specified, Nping will alternate between them in round-robin fashion.

Note: *You must specify --tcp or --udp as the -p option does not work with ICMP pings.*

Perform an ARP Ping

The --arp option allows you to execute an ARP ping.

Usage syntax: nping --arp [target]

```
# nping -c 1 --arp 192.168.1.104

Starting Nping 0.6.47 ( http://nmap.org/nping ) at 2015-01-24 22:23
CST
SENT (0.0042s) ARP who has 192.168.1.104? Tell 192.168.1.100
RCVD (0.0078s) ARP reply 192.168.1.104 is at 34:17:EB:D3:57:CD

Max rtt: N/A | Min rtt: N/A | Avg rtt: N/A
Raw packets sent: 1 (42B) | Rcvd: 1 (46B) | Lost: 0 (0.00%)
Nping done: 1 IP address pinged in 1.01 seconds
```

Performing an ARP ping

On local Ethernet networks, IP addresses are converted to network interface MAC (Media Access Control) addresses using ARP (Address Resolution Protocol). This facilitates transmission of data via layer 2 switches. The --arp option utilizes this fundamental feature of Ethernet to let you send an ARP broadcast to ping a host, as shown in the example above. This is useful in situations where a system on the local network runs firewall software that drops unsolicited ICMP, TCP, and UDP traffic. This system will not respond to any pings but it must reply to ARP broadcasts.

To illustrate this case, the same host from the above example is pinged 3 different ways below for comparison.

```
# ping -c 3 192.168.1.104
PING 192.168.1.104 (192.168.1.104): 56 data bytes
Request timeout for icmp_seq 0
Request timeout for icmp_seq 1
Request timeout for icmp_seq 2

--- 192.168.1.104 ping statistics ---
3 packets transmitted, 0 packets received, 100.0% packet loss

# nping -H 192.168.1.104

Starting Nping 0.6.47 ( http://nmap.org/nping ) at 2015-01-24 22:18
CST

Max rtt: N/A | Min rtt: N/A | Avg rtt: N/A
Raw packets sent: 5 (140B) | Rcvd: 0 (0B) | Lost: 5 (100.00%)
Nping done: 1 IP address pinged in 5.02 seconds

# nping -H -tcp 192.168.1.104

Starting Nping 0.6.47 ( http://nmap.org/nping ) at 2015-01-24 22:19
CST
```

```
Max rtt: N/A | Min rtt: N/A | Avg rtt: N/A
Raw packets sent: 5 (200B) | Rcvd: 0 (0B) | Lost: 5 (100.00%)
Nping done: 1 IP address pinged in 5.01 seconds
```

In each case, the host refused to respond due to firewall software running on the system. By using ARP, we can bypass the firewall and check its liveliness (and also discover its MAC address in the process).

Miscellaneous Nping Options

In the interest of keeping this book "fat-free," some less common options are listed below rather than giving them their own usage recipe. A few of these have practical uses (like -d for debug and -6 for ipv6) but were skipped because their Nmap counterparts were covered earlier.

-h
Display Nping help

-V
Display Nping version

-d[level]
Set debug level (1 to 6)

-v[level]
Set verbosity level (-4 to 4)

-e [interface]
Use the specified network interface

-g [port]
Spoof the specified source port

--flags [flags]
Use the specified TCP flags

-6 [address]
Ping the specified IPv6 address

--echo-server [passphrase]
Setup an echo server for use with the --echo-client option

--echo-client [passphrase]
Ping an echo server

Tip: *The options discussed in this book cover everyday usage. There are many other obscure uses available for Nping. The nping manual is an excellent resource for additional information on these features. You can read the man page on Unix/Linux/Mac by executing man nping. Windows users can visit nmap.org/book/nping-man.html to read the manual online.*

Section 15: Ncat

Overview

Ncat is another new addition to the Nmap suite. Beginning with Nmap 5, Ncat was released as a modern replacement for the popular Netcat program that is no longer actively developed. Ncat is designed to be a "Swiss Army Knife" for all things TCP/IP. You can use Ncat to act as a client or server for virtually any type of service or protocol. This allows you to see and manipulate raw protocol behavior in real-time, which can be useful for troubleshooting or security auditing.

Note: *Ncat is a complex tool that has countless uses. I could come up with enough material to write a whole book just on this one utility. Unfortunately, this is not that book. This guide is written from a network administrator's point of view. As such, it only covers basic usage of the utility for testing and troubleshooting. This section covers the basic operation of Ncat and it's up to you to find creative uses for the tool.*

Summary of features covered in this section:

Test a Webserver

Test a SMTP Server

Transfer a File

Create an Ad Hoc Chat Server

Create an Ad Hoc Webserver

Test a Webserver

Using Ncat to connect to port 80 or 443 on a webserver allows you to test the functionality of the system by issuing HTTP requests.

Usage syntax (HTTP): ncat -C [target] 80

Usage syntax (SSL): ncat -C --ssl [target] 443

```
$ ncat 192.168.1.103 80

HEAD / HTTP/1.0 <ENTER><ENTER>

HTTP/1.1 200 OK
Date: Sun, 25 Jan 2015 06:23:33 GMT
Server: Apache/2.4.7 (Ubuntu)
Last-Modified: Sun, 25 Jan 2015 06:08:46 GMT
ETag: "2cf6-50d73dac8beb2"
Accept-Ranges: bytes
Content-Length: 11510
Vary: Accept-Encoding
Connection: close
Content-Type: text/html
<CTRL + D>
```

Output of a webserver test using ncat

Using Ncat can be helpful when testing webserver configuration without having to open a browser or clear caches. It can also show you HTTP headers from the server (demonstrated above) which browsers normally hide from end users. In this example, Ncat connects to a web server on port 80. The HTTP request "**HEAD / HTTP/1.0**" is issued (followed by hitting the <ENTER> key twice) which displays some basic information about the server. The command "**GET / HTTP/1.0**" could also be issued to dump the HTML contents of the server's index page to the screen. When finished, pressing <CTRL + D> ends the session.

Note: *Some webservers may require adding the -C option when connecting to send proper CRLF line endings.*

Ncat can be especially helpful when testing virtual hosting configuration. On vhosts, additional information is required in order to form a proper HTTP request. The next example displays the syntax for testing a virtual webserver.

```
$ ncat www.example.com.com 80
GET / HTTP/1.0
HOST: www.example.com <ENTER><ENTER>
[...]
```

Testing a virtual hosted system

Test a SMTP Server

Another neat use for Ncat is testing a SMTP (Simple Mail Transfer Protocol) server.

Usage syntax: ncat [target] 25

```
$ ncat 192.168.1.103 25
220 E6420 ESMTP Postfix (Ubuntu)
HELO test
250 E6420
QUIT
221 2.0.0 Bye

<CTRL + D>
```

Testing a SMTP server connection

Connecting to a SMTP server on port 25 allows you to see and interact with a mail server. This is helpful if you are trying to troubleshoot problems with mail systems. You could actually use Ncat in this situation to craft a complete message and send it, assuming you have relay access from your location and understand proper SMTP command syntax.

In the example above, the Ncat client connects to port 25 on the SMTP server and is greeted with a 220 banner displaying some basic information about the server. Issuing the command "HELO test" results in a 250 response from the server. These responses indicate the server is working properly. Once we are satisfied that the server is working we issue the "QUIT" command and then see a 221 message which ends the session. Pressing <CTRL + D> then causes Ncat to return to the shell.

Transfer a File

Ncat provides a simple way to send a single file to another system on the fly without having to use a client/server protocol like FTP.

Usage syntax (receiver): ncat -l >[output]
Usage syntax (sender): ncat --send-only [target] < [input]

```
# ncat -l > test.png
```

Setting up the receiving system to listen for a file

In the first example, we set up the receiving system to listen for a connection and redirect the output to a file. In this case the file being transferred is test.png. The example below shows the syntax used to send the file with the --send-only option and redirect the test.png file as input.

```
# ncat --send-only 192.168.1.103 < test.png
```

Transferring the file from the sending system

This will transfer the test.png file to the listening system and then close the connection. In a pinch, this can be very handy for sending a file to a remote system quickly.

Tip: *You can use a checksum program such as md5sum (Linux) or md5 (Unix/BSD) to verify the integrity of the transferred file. This command can be found on most Unix/Linux systems, but is not available on Windows.*

Create an Ad Hoc Chat Server

Ncat can also be used as a simple chat server between one or more users.

Usage syntax (host): ncat -l
Usage syntax (guest): ncat [host]

```
# ncat -l
```

Setting up ncat to listen as a host

To setup a chat simply have one user run Ncat in listen mode (as shown above) and then connect from another system (demonstrated below).

```
# ncat 192.168.1.103
Sup?
Nothing
Let's go get some tacos!
Ok, meet me downstairs in 5 min.
:)
<CTRL + D>
```

Connecting to the host system and sending messages

Once connected, you can exchange messages between the two systems. Pressing <CTRL + D> ends the session when you are finished.

Tip: *The --chat option is also provided to help facilitate chats between multiple users. This will give each user a unique ID to help keep conversations straight. Include the --chat option on the listening system to enable this feature.*

Create an Ad Hoc Webserver

Using a simple HTTP response and a few HTML tags, you can get Ncat to act like a webserver.

Usage syntax: ncat --listen [port] < [file]

```
# ncat -l 80 < web.server
```

Setting up Ncat to listen on port 80

In the example above, a file called web.server is used as input for Ncat listening on port 80. The contents of the web.server file are shown below and consist of an HTTP response code and then the minimum amount of HTML code needed to serve up a web page.

```
$ cat web.server
HTTP/1.0 200 OK

<html>
  <body>
    <h1>Hello, world!</h1>
  </body>
</html>
```

Creating a simple HTTP response and HTML document

The resulting web page when accessed from a browser is displayed below.

A web browser accessing the Ad Hoc Ncat webserver

On the listening end, Ncat displays the HTTP request along with the User-Agent information supplied by the client. The output of the client request is shown below.

```
GET / HTTP/1.1
Host: 10.10.4.1
Connection: keep-alive
Accept:
```

```
text/html,application/xhtml+xml,application/xml;q=0.9,image/webp,*/*;
q=0.8
User-Agent: Mozilla/5.0 (Windows NT 6.1; WOW64) AppleWebKit/537.36
(KHTML, like Gecko) Chrome/40.0.2214.91 Safari/537.36
Accept-Encoding: gzip, deflate, sdch
Accept-Language: en-US,en;q=0.8
```

Output of a client request to Ncat

Section 16: Tips and Tricks

Overview

This section provides several helpful tips and tricks for getting the most out of Nmap. It also incorporates the use of third party programs that work in conjunction with Nmap to help you analyze your network.

Summary of topics discussed in this section:

Combine Multiple Options

Display Scan Status

Runtime Interaction

Remotely Scan Your Network

Scanme.Nmap.org

Wireshark

Nmap Online Resources

Combine Multiple Options

If you haven't already noticed, Nmap allows you to combine multiple options to produce a custom scan unique to your needs.

Usage syntax: nmap [options] [target]

```
# nmap --reason -F --open -T3 -O scanme.nmap.org

Starting Nmap 6.47 ( http://nmap.org ) at 2015-01-17 12:58 CST
Nmap scan report for scanme.nmap.org (74.207.244.221)
Host is up, received reset (0.057s latency).
Not shown: 98 closed ports
Reason: 98 resets
PORT    STATE SERVICE REASON
22/tcp  open  ssh     syn-ack
80/tcp  open  http    syn-ack
Aggressive OS guesses: Linux 3.0 - 3.9 (94%), Linux 2.6.32 - 3.1
(93%), Linux 2.6.32 - 2.6.39 (92%), Linux 2.6.39 (91%), Linux 2.6.32
- 3.9 (91%), HP P2000 G3 NAS device (90%), Linux 3.0 (90%), OpenWrt
12.09-rc1 Attitude Adjustment (Linux 3.3 - 3.7) (90%), Linux 3.7
(89%), Linux 3.0 - 3.2 (89%)
No exact OS matches for host (test conditions non-ideal).
Network Distance: 9 hops

OS detection performed. Please report any incorrect results at
http://nmap.org/submit/ .
Nmap done: 1 IP address (1 host up) scanned in 11.49 seconds
```

Combining multiple Nmap options

Combining options is where the real fun begins when using Nmap. In the above example, many different options are combined to produce the desired results. This allows you to create a scan customized to meet your specific needs. As you can see, the possibilities are nearly limitless.

Display Scan Status

The --stats-every option can be used to periodically display the status of the current scan.

Usage syntax: nmap --stats-every [time] [target]

```
# nmap --stats-every 5s 10.10.4.1/24

Starting Nmap 6.47 ( http://nmap.org ) at 2015-01-17 11:43 CST
Stats: 0:00:05 elapsed; 0 hosts completed (0 up), 255 undergoing ARP
Ping Scan
ARP Ping Scan Timing: About 83.92% done; ETC: 11:43 (0:00:01
remaining)
Stats: 0:00:10 elapsed; 88 hosts completed (64 up), 64 undergoing SYN
Stealth Scan
SYN Stealth Scan Timing: About 8.56% done; ETC: 11:44 (0:00:53
remaining)
Stats: 0:00:15 elapsed; 88 hosts completed (64 up), 64 undergoing SYN
Stealth Scan
SYN Stealth Scan Timing: About 10.56% done; ETC: 11:45 (0:01:25
remaining)
Stats: 0:00:20 elapsed; 88 hosts completed (64 up), 64 undergoing SYN
Stealth Scan
SYN Stealth Scan Timing: About 12.76% done; ETC: 11:45 (0:01:43
remaining)
Stats: 0:00:25 elapsed; 88 hosts completed (64 up), 64 undergoing SYN
Stealth Scan
SYN Stealth Scan Timing: About 14.56% done; ETC: 11:46 (0:01:57
remaining)
Stats: 0:00:30 elapsed; 88 hosts completed (64 up), 64 undergoing SYN
Stealth Scan
SYN Stealth Scan Timing: About 16.04% done; ETC: 11:46 (0:02:11
remaining)
[...]
```

Nmap scan status output

On slow scans you may get bored looking at your screen doing nothing for long periods of time. The --stats-every option can alleviate this problem. Enabling this option will show the status of the current scan with updates at the specified interval. In the above example, --stats-every 5s instructs Nmap to display the status of the current scan every five seconds. Timing parameters can be specified in seconds (s), minutes (m), or hours (h) by appending an s/m/h qualifier to the interval number.

Runtime Interaction

Nmap offers several runtime interaction keystrokes that can modify a scan in progress. The table below lists Nmap's runtime interaction keys.

v
Pressing lowercase v during a scan will increase the verbosity level.

V
Pressing uppercase V during a scan will decrease the verbosity level.

d
Pressing lowercase d during a scan will increase the debugging level.

D
Pressing uppercase D during a scan will decrease the debugging level.

p
Pressing lowercase p during a scan will enable packet tracing.

P
Pressing uppercase P during a scan will disable packet tracing.

?
Pressing ? during a scan will display the runtime interaction help.

Any other key not listed above
Pressing any key other than the ones defined above during a scan will print a status message indicating the progress of the scan and how much time is remaining.

Nmap runtime interaction keys

Runtime interaction is very useful for getting status updates when performing a scan on a large number of hosts. The example below displays the status of the current scan when the space bar is pressed. The v key is also demonstrated to enable verbose output for the scan in progress.

```
# nmap 10.10.4.1/24

Starting Nmap 6.47 ( http://nmap.org ) at 2015-01-17 13:08 CST

<space>
Stats: 0:00:00 elapsed; 0 hosts completed (0 up), 255 undergoing ARP
Ping Scan
ARP Ping Scan Timing: About 15.10% done; ETC: 13:08 (0:00:06
remaining)

<v>
Verbosity Increased to 1.
```

```
Discovered open port 135/tcp on 10.10.4.103
Discovered open port 80/tcp on 10.10.4.31
Discovered open port 8080/tcp on 10.10.4.43
[...]
```

Using runtime interaction keys to display scan status and verbose output

Remotely Scan Your Network

Nmap Online is a website that provides "free as in beer" Nmap scanning functionality via a web browser. This can be useful for remotely scanning your network or troubleshooting connectivity problems from an external source. Simply visit nmap-online.com, enter your IP address, and select the scan options to suit your needs.

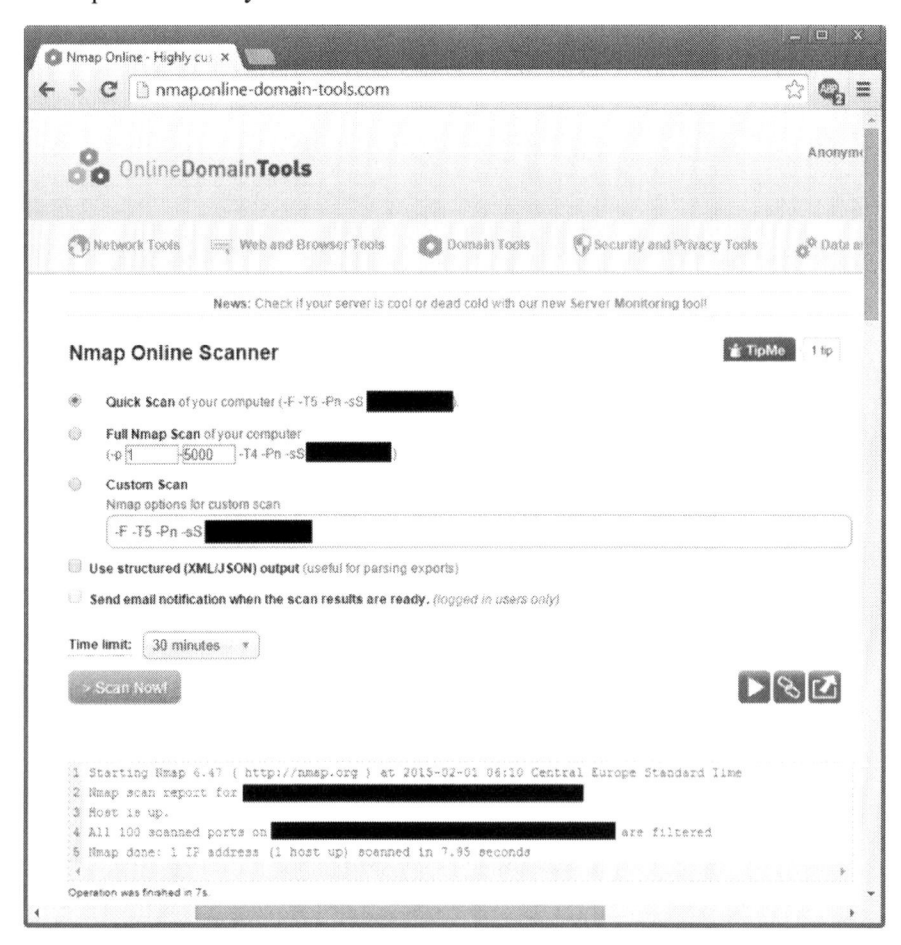

Nmap-online.com home page

Note: *This is a neat service that works well, but the website has become somewhat ad-laden over the years.*

Scanme.Nmap.org

The scanme.nmap.org server is a common example target used throughout this guide. This system is hosted by the Nmap project and can be freely scanned by Nmap users.

```
# nmap -F scanme.nmap.org

Starting Nmap 6.47 ( http://nmap.org ) at 2015-01-17 13:25 CST
Nmap scan report for scanme.nmap.org (74.207.244.221)
Host is up (0.082s latency).
Not shown: 98 closed ports
PORT    STATE SERVICE
22/tcp  open  ssh
80/tcp  open  http

Nmap done: 1 IP address (1 host up) scanned in 2.28 seconds
```

Example scan using scanme.nmap.org as the target

Note: *The good people of the Nmap project provide this valuable service as an educational and troubleshooting tool. They request that you be polite by not aggressively scanning it hundreds of times a day or with other tools not related to Nmap.*

Wireshark

Wireshark is an excellent addition to any system administrator's toolkit. It is a sophisticated (yet easy to use) network protocol analyzer. You can use Wireshark to capture and analyze network traffic and it works hand-in-hand with Nmap by allowing you to see each packet sent and received while scanning.

Wireshark network protocol analyzer

Wireshark is available for Windows, Linux, and Mac OS X and can be downloaded for free at wireshark.org.

Nmap Online Resources

Fyodor's Nmap Book
nmap.org/book/man.html

Nmap Install Guide
nmap.org/book/install.html

Nmap Scripting Engine Documentation
nmap.org/nsedoc/

Zenmap Reference Guide
nmap.org/book/zenmap.html

Nmap Change Log
nmap.org/changelog.html

Nmap Mailing Lists
seclists.org

Nmap GitHub Issue Tracker
github.com/nmap/nmap/issues

Nmap Online Scan
nmap-online.com

Nmap Security Tools Guide
sectools.org

Nmap Facebook
nmap.org/fb

Nmap Twitter
twitter.com/nmap

Nmap Cookbook
nmapcookbook.com

Conclusion

Nmap started as a simple port scanner and has grown into a full suite of network utilities. It is a powerful tool with hundreds of potential option combinations, but it can be used by anyone from the casual administrator to a full-blown security auditor. The Nmap suite can now be used for discovering (nmap), troubleshooting (ncat), and even stress testing (nping). Nmap is a highly valuable tool, yet they give it away for free in the spirit of open source software.

In recent news, many large companies have suffered embarrassing security breaches. Many of these breaches could have been prevented. Nmap is a great tool that you can use to evaluate your presence on the Internet and ensure that your home or business isn't the next target. Security, however, is more than just running an occasional scan on your network. Your TCP/UDP ports are your windows to the world. On the Internet, billions of people around the globe are only milliseconds away from peeking into those windows. Security requires constant monitoring and proactive measures. You must be diligent in keeping your software updated and use "best practices" in configuring your systems to stay one step ahead of the attackers.

Finally, as an administrator, you must always remember that security is an arms race. Whatever tools you are using to monitor your network, attackers are also using, plus many more.

Credits and References

The bulk of my research for this book was performed using the wealth of Nmap's online documentation. This includes mailing lists, man pages, and official Nmap documentation. The Nmap project is one of the most well documented open source projects I have ever come across and I am grateful for their diligent work in providing materials that were referenced during the creation of The Nmap Cookbook.

nmap.org/docs.html

Much of my knowledge of TCP/IP comes from on the job experience. I also received training at the Cisco Networking Academy in preparation for taking the CCNA exam. Cisco provides an excellent training program that goes well beyond simply covering how to use their products. The complete CCNA program covers TCP/IP fundamentals and provides core networking knowledge that is useful outside of the Cisco realm.

netacad.com

Despite my training and on-the-job experience, I could never dream of understanding the IP Suite as well as the people involved with Nmap. To help fill in the gaps, I utilized the information in various IETF RFC documents and Wikipedia entries related to the IP Protocol Suite during the writing of this book. The links below are an excellent starting point for those wanting to dig deeper into TCP/IP to take their understanding to the next level.

en.wikipedia.org/wiki/Internet_protocol_suite

ietf.org/rfc.html

Appendix A - Nmap Cheat Sheet

Download and print this cheat sheet online at *NmapCookbook.com*

Basic Scanning Techniques

Scan a Single Target
nmap [target]

Scan Multiple Targets
nmap [target1, target2, etc]

Scan a Range of Hosts
nmap [range of ip addresses]

Scan an Entire Subnet
nmap [ip address/cidr]

Scan a List of Targets
nmap -iL [list.txt]

Excluding Targets from a Scan
nmap [targets] --exclude [targets]

Excluding Targets Using a List
nmap [targets] --excludefile [list.txt]

Scan Random Hosts
nmap -iR [number]

Perform an Aggressive Scan
nmap -A [target]

Scan an IPv6 Target
nmap -6 [target]

Periodically Display Statistics
nmap --stats-every [time] [target]

Discovery Options

Perform a Ping Only Scan
nmap -sn [target]

Don't Ping
nmap -Pn [target]

TCP SYN Ping
nmap -PS [target]

TCP ACK Ping
nmap -PA [target]

UDP Ping
nmap -PU [target]

ICMP Echo Ping
nmap -PE [target]

ICMP Timestamp Ping
nmap -PP [target]

ICMP Address Mask Ping
nmap -PM [target]

IP Protocol Ping
nmap -PO [target]

ARP Ping
nmap -PR [target]

Traceroute
nmap --traceroute [target]

Force Reverse DNS Resolution
nmap -R [target]

Disable Reverse DNS Resolution
nmap -n [target]

Alternative DNS Lookup
nmap --system-dns [target]

Manually Specify DNS Server(s)
nmap --dns-servers [servers] [target]

Create a Host List
nmap -sL [targets]

<u>**Advanced Scanning Functions**</u>

TCP SYN Scan
nmap -sS [target]

TCP Connect Scan
nmap -sT [target]

UDP Scan
nmap -sU [target]

TCP NULL Scan
nmap -sN [target]

TCP FIN Scan
nmap -sF [target]

Xmas Scan
nmap -sX [target]

TCP ACK Scan
nmap -sA [target]

Custom TCP Scan
nmap --scanflags [flags] [target]

IP Protocol Scan
nmap -sO [target]

Port Scanning Options

Perform a Fast Scan
nmap -F [target]

Scan Specific Ports
nmap -p [port(s)] [target]

Scan Ports by Name
nmap -p [port name(s)] [target]

Scan Ports by Protocol
nmap -sU -sT -p U:[ports],T:[ports] [target]

Scan All Ports
nmap -p "*" [target]

Scan Top Ports
nmap --top-ports [number] [target]

Perform a Sequential Port Scan
nmap -r [target]

Only Display Open Ports
nmap --open [target]

Version Detection

Operating System Detection
nmap -O [target]

Submit TCP/IP Fingerprints

nmap.org/submit/

Attempt to Guess an Unknown OS
nmap -O --osscan-guess [target]

Service Version Detection
nmap -sV [target]

Troubleshooting Version Scans
nmap -sV --version-trace [target]

Timing Options

Timing Templates
nmap -T[0-5] [target]

Set the Packet TTL
nmap --ttl [time] [target]

Minimum # of Parallel Operations
nmap --min-parallelism [number] [target]

Maximum # of Parallel Operations
nmap --max-parallelism [number] [target]

Minimum Host Group Size
nmap --min-hostgroup [number] [targets]

Maximum Host Group Size
nmap --max-hostgroup [number] [targets]

Maximum RTT Timeout
nmap --initial-rtt-timeout [time] [target]

Initial RTT Timeout
nmap --max-rtt-timeout [TTL] [target]

Maximum Retries
nmap --max-retries [number] [target]

Host Timeout
nmap --host-timeout [time] [target]

Minimum Scan Delay
nmap --scan-delay [time] [target]

Maximum Scan Delay
nmap --max-scan-delay [time] [target]

Minimum Packet Rate

nmap --min-rate [number] [target]

Maximum Packet Rate
nmap --max-rate [number] [target]

Defeat Reset Rate Limits
nmap --defeat-rst-ratelimit [target]

Firewall Evasion Techniques

Fragment Packets
nmap -f [target]

Specify a Specific MTU
nmap --mtu [MTU] [target]

Use a Decoy
nmap -D RND:[number] [target]

Idle Zombie Scan
nmap -sI [zombie] [target]

Manually Specify a Source Port
nmap --source-port [port] [target]

Append Random Data
nmap --data-length [size] [target]

Randomize Target Scan Order
nmap --randomize-hosts [target]

Spoof MAC Address
nmap --spoof-mac [MAC|0|vendor] [target]

Send Bad Checksums
nmap --badsum [target]

Output Options

Save Output to a Text File
nmap -oN [scan.txt] [target]

Save Output to a XML File
nmap -oX [scan.xml] [target]

Grepable Output
nmap -oG [scan.txt] [targets]

Output All Supported File Types
nmap -oA [path/filename] [target]

133t Output
nmap -oS [scan.txt] [target]

Troubleshooting and Debugging

Getting Help
nmap -h

Display Nmap Version
nmap -V

Verbose Output
nmap -v [target]

Debugging
nmap -d [target]

Display Port State Reason
nmap --reason [target]

Trace Packets
nmap --packet-trace [target]

Display Host Networking
nmap --iflist

Specify a Network Interface
nmap -e [interface] [target]

Nmap Scripting Engine

Execute Individual Scripts
nmap --script [script.nse] [target]

Execute Multiple Scripts
nmap --script [expression] [target]

Script Categories
all, auth, default, discovery, external, intrusive, malware, safe, vuln

Execute Scripts by Category
nmap --script [category] [target]

Execute Multiple Script Categories
nmap --script [category1,category2,etc]

Troubleshoot Scripts
nmap --script [script] --script-trace [target]

Update the Script Database

nmap --script-updatedb

Ndiff

Comparison Using Ndiff
ndiff [scan1.xml] [scan2.xml]

Ndiff Verbose Mode
ndiff -v [scan1.xml] [scan2.xml]

XML Output Mode
ndiff --xml [scan1.xml] [scan2.xml]

Nping

Ping a Target
nping [target]

Ping Multiple Targets
nping [target1 target 2 etc.]

Hide sent packets
nping -H [target]

Hide All Packets
nping -q [target]

Specify a Ping Count
nping -c [count] [target]

Specify a Ping Rate
nping --rate [rate] [target]

Specify a Ping Delay
nping --delay [delay] [target]

Generate a Payload
nping --data-length [length] [target]

Ping Using TCP
nping --tcp [target]

Ping Using UDP
nping --udp [target]

Ping a Specific Port
nping -p [port] --tcp|--udp [target]

Perform an ARP ping
nping --arp [target]

Display Nping Help
nping -h

Display Nping Version
nping -V

Set Debug Level (1 to 6)
nping -d[level] [target]

Set verbosity level (-4 to 4)
nping -v[level] [target]

Use the Specified Network Interface
nping -e [interface] [target]

Spoof the Specified Source Port
nping -g [port] [target]

Use the Specified TCP Flags
nping --flags [flags] [target]

Ping the Specified IPv6 Address
nping -6 [target]

Setup an Echo Server
nping --echo-server [passphrase]

Ping an Echo Server
nping --echo-client [passphrase] [target]

Ncat

Connect to an Address/port
ncat [address] [port]

Use SSL
ncat --ssl [address] [port]

Listen for Incoming Connections
ncat --listen [port]

Appendix B - Miscellaneous Nmap Options

In the interest of being a complete (but also fat-free) guide to Nmap, the rarely used options listed here are not covered in this book but are mentioned below for your reference.

--nsock-engine
Specify a specific nsock engine (see nmap -V for a list of available engines)

--resume
Resume an aborted scan (requires -oN or -oG logs)

--port-ratio
Scan ports in the nmap-services file greater than the specified ratio

--datadir
Override the default Nmap data directory

--servicedb
Override the default nmap-services file

--versiondb
Override the default nmap-service-probes file

--privileged
Assume that the user has the required privileges for raw socket sniffing

--unprivileged
Assume that the user does not have the required privileges for raw socket sniffing

--release-memory
Used for memory leak debugging

--send-eth
Instructs Nmap to use raw ethernet frames while scanning

--send-ip
Instructs Nmap to use IP packets while scanning

--ip-options
Specify IP options in IP packets

-S
Spoof the specified IP address

--proxies

223

Use an HTTP or SOCKS4 proxy for TCP connections (this feature is still under development)

-sY
Perform an SCTP INIT scan

-sZ
Perform a SCTP COOKIE ECHO scan

-PY
Perform an SCTP INIT Ping

--adler32
Calculate SCTP checksums using Adler32 algorithm

-sW
Perform a TCP Window scan.

-sM
Perform a TCP Maimon scan

-R
Force reverse DNS lookup

Ready to learn the command line?

Check out our latest title...

Introduction to the Command Line is a practical guide that teaches the most important Unix and Linux shell commands in a simple and straightforward manner. All command line programs covered are presented with visual examples to aid in the learning process and help you master the command line quickly and easily.

FatFreePublishing.com

Printed in Great Britain
by Amazon